The Very Easy Guide to Using Your Sewing Machine

Wendy Gardiner

SEARCH PRESS

First published in Great Britain 2014

Search Press Limited
Wellwood, North Farm Road,
Tunbridge Wells, Kent TN2 3DR

Text copyright © Wendy Gardiner 2014

Photographs by Paul Bricknell at Search Press Studios

Photographs and design copyright © Search Press Ltd 2014

ISBN: 978-1-84448-828-5

Suppliers

If you have difficulty in obtaining any of the materials and
equipment mentioned in this book, then please visit the Search
Press website for details of suppliers: www.searchpress.com

You are invited to visit the author's website: www.isew.co.uk and
follow her blog: http://blog.sew.co.uk/author/wendy/

For more information on Toyota home sewing machines go to
www.home-sewing.com

Helpline: 08705 133106

> **Publisher's note**
>
> All the step-by-step photographs in this book feature
> the author, Wendy Gardiner, demonstrating how to use
> a sewing machine. No models have been used.

Printed in China

Acknowledgements

With thanks to Toyota for providing the lovely
sewing machines with which to make all the
projects and samples. Thanks also to
Art Gallery Fabrics for the beautiful cotton
fabrics supplied through Hantex Ltd
(www.hantex.co.uk/agf) and to Madeira for
the threads. A special thanks to my boys
(husband Lez and sons Jake and Charlie) who
put up with me sewing, snipping, clipping and
pressing to all hours!

THE VERY EASY GUIDE
TO USING YOUR
SEWING MACHINE

Foreword by Toyota

In 1946 when Mr Toyoda created the first Toyota sewing machine and incidentally the first Toyota car, quality, beauty and simplicity were at the forefront of his design principles.

As we move forward almost 70 years, those principles still remain. 'Simply created to make things beautiful' is the phrase that defines our sewing machines.

Customer usability is another vital aspect of our sewing machines. We want everyone who has a Toyota sewing machine to be able to use the machine to its full potential and to see it as a valued part of their daily lives, and not a scary object that lives in the loft or under the stairs!

We wanted to create a book that did not expect Toyota sewists to know immediately what they were doing, and one which would take the mystique and fear out of sewing. When we first discussed the prospect of creating such a book with Search Press and with our author, Wendy Gardiner, we were delighted to discover that they held the same vision, and we would like to express our sincere thanks for their hard work and dedication in creating *The Very Easy Guide to Using Your Sewing Machine*.

In our view, this book not only achieves our original concept, but goes beyond that by encouraging sewists to learn, improve and develop their sewing skills.

We hope that you enjoy reading this book and that it helps you to be inspired to get the most out of your Toyota sewing machine and to create beautiful things. After all, this is what Mr Toyoda had in mind from the very beginning.

TOYOTA SEWING MACHINES

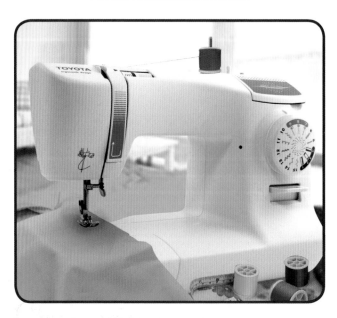

CONTENTS

INTRODUCTION

When Toyota and Search Press first asked me to write a book on basic sewing for beginners, I felt as if all my wishes had come true in one go! I love to sew, particularly by machine and am always keen to share my passion for fabric, thread, haberdashery and lovely modern sewing machines. I really enjoy seeing the light bulb moment when new sewists realise they can do it, and that it is fun, affordable and rewarding.

So this book encompasses it all, from getting the machine out of the box to creating projects that you can be proud of. I have demystified the knobs, dials and threading system, showing that whatever machine you have, the basic principles are the same.

Throughout the book there are tips and hints to make sewing easier as well as how-to steps for all the basic sewing techniques you might need to create your own fashions or furnishings. To help you get to grips with the techniques, there is a series of pretty and practical projects for you to sew, which will also help you become fully acquainted with your machine and confident to tackle any project you want. We start with handy drawstring bags that are made with simple straight stitching and then move on to add zigzag and decorative stitches, ending with some creative work 'drawing with thread' as you sew your own free-motion designs on a chiffon scarf. As you gain confidence, you can move on to making an apron using twin needles, and decorating a towel with bobbin work. Once you have mastered the more advanced techniques at the end of the book, there will be no looking back, and you and your sewing machine will be able to take on any number of exciting projects.

Of course, there are times when things go wrong and your stitching isn't perfect. It happens to us all, so together with Toyota, I have put together a very comprehensive Troubleshooting guide that will help you solve any stitch problems you encounter (see page 119).

So let's start at the very beginning. When you are starting off with a new sewing machine, put the box on a flat surface. Gently turn it on its side or upside down and gradually slide out the polystyrene case. Then take off the tape which holds the polystyrene together and gently open the case. Lift the machine out carefully, watching out for any sharp or loose items that may fall out. I always recommend keeping the box and inner packaging in a safe place so that you can use it when sending the machine for servicing. Read the instruction manual before beginning to sew as it will include some great sewing tips, and keep it in a safe place to refer to as needed.

I do hope you enjoy working your way through this book and find that you love to sew as much as I do.

Happy sewing!

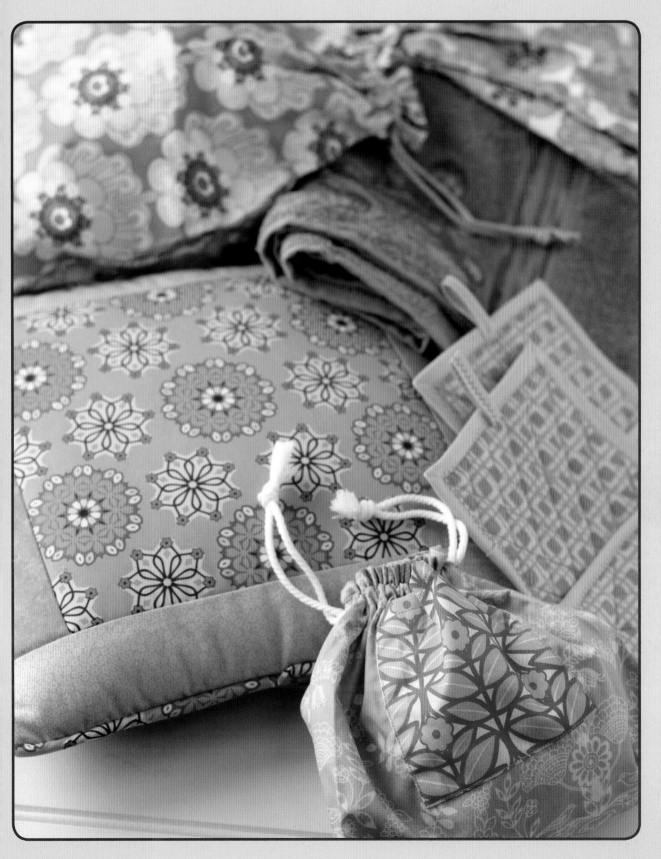

YOUR SEWING MACHINE

This is a quick guide to what's what on your sewing machine. It explains the knobs, dials and basic functions so that you can confidently start to sew. The basic components of a sewing machine are generally in the same place and although different models may have more or fewer special functions, which will depend on make and price, it is comforting to know that once you have identified the basics, you can do so on almost any machine.

Balance wheel (fly wheel/hand wheel)

This is the large round knob on the right-hand side of the machine. It is used to lower and raise the needle by hand. Always turn the wheel towards yourself. On inexpensive machines, this wheel may have a separate outer ring or switch on it which is used to disengage the needle when winding bobbins.

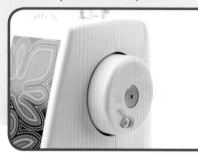

Bobbin winding spindle

A short spindle on the top right of the machine on to which the bobbin is placed ready to be wound. You may have to push the spindle across to engage it, or push a lever next to it towards the bobbin. On most machines, moving the spindle or lever will disengage the needle when bobbin winding, but if not, check the balance wheel as mentioned above. Most bobbins will only wind until they are full and then automatically stop. For full instructions, see page 24.

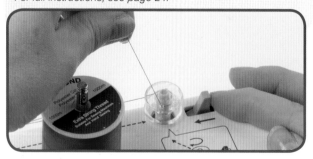

Bobbin

Lots of machines have a drop-in bobbin in front of the needle (see right). Drop-in bobbins are very easy to use, have a clear plastic cover and are often made from clear plastic themselves, so it is easy to see at a glance how much thread is left. There is often a little diagram on the plastic cover or next to the bobbin casing showing the threading direction.

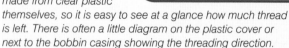

The other type is the front-loading bobbin (see right). If you can't find your bobbin in front of the needle, under the plastic cover, it's a front loader!

See page 25 for instructions on inserting both types of bobbin.

Tip

Although all bobbins look the same, they can vary slightly in size and thus fit. Use bobbins intended for your model/make of machine to avoid problems.

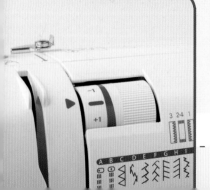

Tension dial

The top thread tension is set by a dial on the front or top of the machine, usually just above the needle area. It is numbered and will usually have the most common or default tension highlighted in some way – by darker numbers, or circled numbers. Generally leave the tension set at the default position as most modern machines stitch perfectly well on all types of fabric. If you do adjust the tension, do so a little at a time. Perfect stitches are formed with the top thread visible on the top of the fabric, and the bobbin thread on the underside.

Top thread spindle

Place the thread reel on the spindle, which may be vertical (see left) or horizontal, depending on the make and model. On a horizontal spindle it is essential to add the thread retainer (a round disk with a hole in centre which fits on the spindle) to hold the reel in place. This will stop the reel sliding along the spindle as you stitch, to help prevent the threads wrapping around the spindle and snagging, which can result in skipped or even broken stitching as the thread unravels unevenly.

Many machines come with a spare spindle in the tool kit. This is useful for top stitching with two threads going through the needle for greater definition, and for twin needle stitching (see right). The second spindle will fit into a hole on the top of the machine, or on to the bobbin spindle.

For instructions on upper threading, see pages 26–27.

Tip

If you only have one spindle but want to use two threads, wind a spare bobbin and place on the one spindle with the thread reel.

Needle threader

Many modern machines have a needle threader which is a real boon when threading the eye of the needle. Most are on the left of the machine, with a lever that you pull down. The thread is pulled through the eye of the needle by a tiny hook on the arm of the needle threader, which is almost impossible to see. If it doesn't work, try raising the needle so that the arm of the threader is in line with the needle eye. For full instructions, see page 27.

To thread a needle without a needle threader, hold a scrap of white paper behind the eye which makes it much more visible and easy to thread.

Needle

Your machine will come with a standard universal needle already fitted. But it will need changing regularly – after every eight hours of sewing or every sewing project. Machine needles have a flat section on the shank, which is usually placed 'flat to back' of the machine when fitted up into the needle socket. See page 18 for how to change a needle.

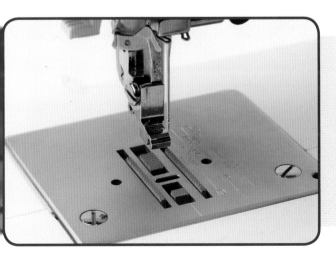

Throat plate

This is the metal plate below the needle with holes for the feed dogs (see below) and the needle. It often also has markings to the right of the needle which can be used to maintain straight seams. The marking will be the distance the needle is from the fabric edge if the edge is placed along the mark.

Feed dogs

The little teeth that protrude through the throat plate are the feed dogs. They move up and down as you sew, helping to move the fabric through (see left).

Presser foot

The basic purpose of a presser foot is to hold the fabric flat while it is being sewn. Most machines come with a few different feet for specific sewing techniques and they will vary in shape, or have attachments to help with different techniques such as zip insertion, blind hemming or overcasting. Most machines now have snap-on or clip-on presser feet which are easy to remove; press a little button behind the foot and it will drop off. To attach a new foot, position it under the foot holder which has a groove on the underside. Line up the horizontal pin on the foot with the groove and lower the presser foot lever to snap on the foot.

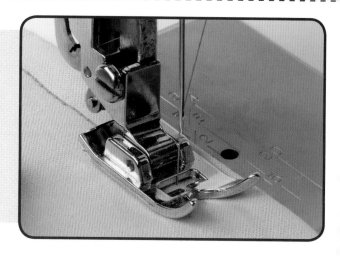

Presser foot lever

This is located behind the needle at the back of the machine and lowered and raised with the right hand. Make sure it is raised when threading and lowered to sew. There is often an option to hold it up a littler higher to insert thick fabric layers under the needle. Just push it up a little more and hold as you insert the fabrics.

Presser foot pressure adjustor

Some machines have a knob or dial located on the left of the machine (on the top, side or back) with which to adjust the pressure of the presser foot. It will have been set to general sewing when it leaves the factory, but if you wish to sew particularly light or heavy fabrics, it can be adjusted to help feed the fabrics evenly. For lightweight or stretchy fabrics, a reduced pressure is required, so turn the dial towards the '–' (or minus) sign.

Flat bed/free arm/extension table

All machines have what is termed a flat bed – that is the surface area around the needle which helps hold fabric flat as it is sewn. Most convert to free arm by taking part of the flat bed away (see right). This extension may be clipped to the front or back or wrapped round the front, back and side. It frequently holds the tools tray too. Converting to free arm means you can stitch small areas such as cuffs, sleeves and trouser legs more easily.

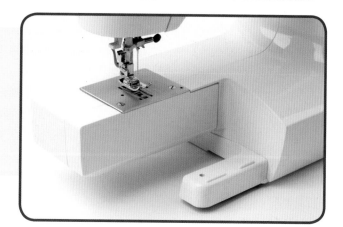

Reverse stitching button/lever

All machines have a lever or button which you hold down to continue stitching in reverse. When you let go, the machine reverts to forward stitching. The button is often on the lower right of the machine (as shown right), but sometimes it is located close to the needle. It will have a U-turn arrow to indicate its use.

Tip

Rather than starting to sew at the very end of the fabric, start about 2cm (³/₄in) in, take two or three stitches, then hold down the reverse button and stitch backwards to the fabric end, before continuing forwards. This secures the stitching and prevents the fabric from tangling or being pulled into the feed dogs at the start.

Stitch selection

Most machines have the choice of stitches printed either on the front of the machine, or on the inside of the flap covering the thread spindle. The stitch choices will be identified in a way which corresponds to numbers, letters or pictures on the stitch selection dial. Make sure the needle is raised before changing the stitch choice, as it will move from side to side as you make the change.

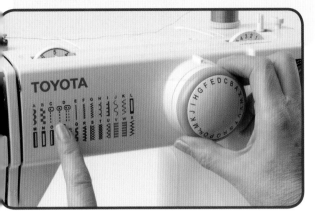

Stitch width and length dials/buttons

These dials or buttons are used to alter the width and length of the chosen stitch. Not all machines have both additional options; more basic machines will just have the set stitch selection, but some will have a choice of stitch length as well. A standard stitch length for most purposes is 2.2–2.5mm (13). Use a longer stitch for multiple layers or bulky fabrics. Stitch width is used for all sideways stitches such as zigzag or decorative stitches. The higher the number or wider the printed scale, the longer or wider the stitch.

Extras

As machines increase in price, so they have more functions and facilities. Many of the additional features are conveniently sited just above the needle area, so they are to hand when you are sewing.

Fix/lock stitch button

This is used to stitch on the spot, securing the threads in place and is used instead of reverse stitching.

Sewing speed lever

This is usually a sliding dial that you move to the left to stitch very slowly or to the right to speed up.

Stop/start button

This is used instead of the foot pedal. Try it out on scrap fabric first, as it can make the machine stitch very quickly. Control the speed by using the sewing speed lever. You usually have to unplug the foot pedal to use the stop/start button.

Knee lift

This is used to raise the presser foot without having to take your hands from the work or use the presser foot lever on the machine. It is fitted in a hole at the front of the machine. It takes some practice to coordinate using your knee and stitching!

Machine maintenance

- Make sure you change your needle after every eight hours of sewing, or after every project, particularly when sewing tough fabrics or multiple layers.

- Defluff the machine after every project by removing the bobbin and using the little brush provided to sweep out the fluff. Occasionally you should also unscrew and remove the throat plate, remove the bobbin race and brush out underneath. It gets surprisingly dirty when sewing!

- Many of the new sewing machines are self lubricating so you don't need to oil them. However, they do still need maintenance and servicing.

- Always ensure the needle is in the raised position before changing stitch selection as it will move sideways as you change stitch, and could bend or break if it hits the side of the throat plate.

Basic feet and accessories

Basic/zigzag stitch foot Most machines come with the zigzag or basic foot attached. This has a wide aperture through which the needle fits for both straight sewing and zigzag or decorative stitching. It has two toes towards the front. Use this foot for most general sewing.

Straight stitch foot This has a much smaller hole for the needle in the centre of the foot. This is useful if sewing fine, lightweight fabrics as it helps prevent the fabric bunching up or being pulled into the throat plate by the feed dogs.

Zipper foot This usually has a solid foot facing forward with indents either side and two pins at the back so it can be attached to the machine with the foot to the right or left of the needle. This means you can stitch close to the zip teeth without the foot being in the way. A zipper foot is used to insert zips, but is also very useful for attaching piping and some trims. Some zipper feet have a sliding bar at the back so that the foot can be moved along the bar to get closer to the zip or piping.

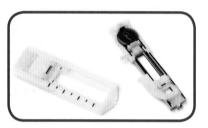

Buttonhole foot This is usually white plastic with markings on the left side and a sliding centre. It has a tiny hook at the rear and two little toes sticking out at the front for creating corded buttonholes, (see page 51). The underside of the foot has a shallow channel through the centre so the foot slides smoothly over the concentrated stitching of a buttonhole. Some buttonhole feet also have a sliding section at the back into which a button can be placed. The foot is then snapped or clipped to the foot holder in the usual way, and the buttonhole stitched to fit the button.

Blind hem foot This has a thicker right toe or bar that protrudes under the foot. This bar is butted up against the fold in the hem allowance when creating a blind hem and ensures a nice straight line. Some blind hem feet come with a little wheel on the right which moves the bar or right toe of the foot so that you can determine how far to the left the zigzag of the blind hem stitch goes (see page 66). You can also use the blind hem foot to 'stitch in the ditch' by running the protruding bar down the previous seamline to stitch right on top of it, making the stitching virtually invisible.

Overcast/overedge foot This may have a little brush on the right of the foot, plus thin metal pins in the centre. The foot is used to stitch right on and indeed over the edge of the fabric while holding the fabric flat as you stitch.

Darning foot This is an optional extra used for free-motion stitching (see page 82). It is a tall foot which is attached to the shank holding the presser foot in place rather than snapped on like other feet. It usually has an oval base with a large hole in the centre and a spring on the shaft of the foot with a little lever to the top right. This lever goes over the needle bar on the sewing machine to help the foot lower and raise as you stitch.

Accessories

Your machine will come with some accessories, which might be hidden away in the front of the free arm section.

Spare bobbins Use bobbins that are made for your machine to ensure they fit properly. Although bobbins all look the same, they can differ slightly in size and thickness.

Seam ripper This is a most useful tool! It has a prong at one end with a razor sharp blade in the inner curve. It is used to unpick stitching but also to open buttonholes. A seam ripper will blunt over time and should be replaced.

Screwdriver tool This may be an actual little screwdriver or a flat, shaped metal tool. It is used to loosen and tighten the screws holding the needle and foot holder in place, and the throat plate. Always use the screwdriver to tighten screws one more twist so that the parts cannot work loose as you stitch.

Thread retainer/spool cap A disc with a central hole used to keep thread reels from bouncing up and down the spindle as you sew. You may have one or two of these. Use the smaller one for the tall, thin reels of thread and the larger one for round thread reels.

Quilting guide This is a metal bar with a curved hook on one end. It is used to help stitch repeated straight parallel lines and is attached to the back of the presser foot holder. It is very useful when quilting or when sewing parallel rows of stitching.

Spare needles Needles are universal but your machine may come with a few handy spares, including a more robust needle for heavyweight fabrics, a ballpoint needle for sewing stretchy fabrics and a twin needle. Remember to replace needles regularly. For more information on needle choice, see pages 18–19.

Walking foot This is a larger, boxy looking foot with its own feed dogs and an arm on the right which goes over the needle holder screw. As the needle goes up and down, so do the feed dogs on the walking foot, so they work in conjunction with the feed dogs on the machine. This means that fabric layers are fed through perfectly together. Use this foot on bulky fabrics or when it is essential to match patterns and stripes.

Oil Some basic machines still come with a little vial of sewing machine oil, though many are now self-lubricating so do not need oiling. If your machine comes with oil, check your user's manual to determine where and how often to add oil.

Clockwise from top: quilting guide, seam ripper, spare spindle, thread retainer, spare bobbins, a variety of feet, screwdriver tool, screwdriver, walking foot, spare needles.

TOOLS AND EQUIPMENT

Essential kit

There are numerous sewing aids and tools to help you sew successfully. These are the 'must-have' items that you will need for all the projects.

Scissors Absolutely essential are good shears for cutting fabric and pattern tissue only. They often have moulded handles that are easier on the hand, particularly with frequent use, and blades angled from the handle so they cut along the table smoothly. If you are left-handed, look for shears designed for you as the moulded handles of right-handed shears will be uncomfortable.

Embroidery scissors Very useful for snipping thread ends and clipping into small areas. Keep a sharp pair in your workbox.

Pinking shears These are really handy for neatening the raw edges of lightweight fabrics such as cottons, felts and linen-like fabrics. The jagged blades cut the fabric with a zigzag edge to prevent fraying without the need for other neatening techniques.

Seam ripper This frequently comes as part of a sewing machine tool kit but will need replacing as the blade will blunt over time. Very useful for unpicking stitching and opening buttonholes.

Needles Keep a selection of hand and machine needles in your workbox. A pack of assorted hand needles will be useful for taking threads to the reverse of the work, sewing on snap fasteners and buttons, hand basting (tacking) and slip stitching turning gaps. A selection of machine needles is also advisable, for lightweight to heavyweight fabrics, stretch fabrics and others. For more on needles, see pages 18–19. Also consider a twin needle (again available for stretch fabrics and woven fabrics) as you get two perfectly formed rows of parallel stitching at the same time. This is great for top stitching, making tiny pin tucks and other decorative stitching.

Pins Like needles, pins need replacing as they blunt over time and will snag fabrics. Good quality, sharp pins are a must. Those with coloured glass heads are useful as they are easy to handle and remove as you sew and of course, can be seen more easily when dropped! Place pins at right angles in the work so you can remove them as you sew. A **magnetic pin holder** is also useful.

Marking tools Have a selection of marking tools to transfer placement lines for buttons, zips and pockets or to mark fold lines for pleats and darts. There is a whole range available from chalk pencils, wheels and blocks to fade-away pens and water soluble pens, which wash out. Generally, mark on the reverse of the fabric whenever possible, and if using a pen, check it doesn't bleed into the fabric by marking on a scrap first.

Tape measure A tape measure with both metric and imperial measurements is very useful. Note, if yours is very old, get a new one as they can stretch over time which means your measuring will not be accurate.

Steam iron Every seam should be pressed before it is sewn over again. Pressing really does make a huge difference in the appearance of a project. A good steam iron will help you ensure your projects look professionally finished.

Point turner This has a point at one end used to turn out corners fully. Many point turners also double as hem markers and pleat markers as they have measurements marked along the edge.

Clockwise from top left: pinking shears, dressmaking scissors, magnetic pin holder, embroidery scissors, pins, pincushion, hand needles, water soluble pen, point turner, chalk pencils, chalk wheel, tape measure and seam ripper.

Other useful items

As well as the essential kit shown on the previous pages, here are some more items on the 'wish list' that make life that little bit easier.

Bias binding maker Raw edges are neatly encased within bias binding and look very professional. It is an easy trim to add, particularly when the bias binding is made using a bias binding maker. These come in different sizes or widths to suit lightweight to heavyweight fabrics and can be used with any fabric. Just cut the fabric into strips twice the width of the bias tape being made and then, working on an ironing board, feed it through the bias binding maker, pressing the folded strips with a hot iron as you pull them through. You can also buy a bias binding machine which feeds the fabric strips, folds and presses them at the touch of a button.

Fabric glue A dab of fabric glue will stop threads unravelling or fabric fraying when cut close to the stitching at curves and V-necklines.

Interfacing This is used to provide support and stability to fabric. It is attached to the reverse side of the fabric and can be an iron-on variety or sew-in. It comes in different weights: light, medium and firm, in white, charcoal and beige and can also be used to stiffen garment areas such as collars and cuffs. Iron-on is quickest to use as you iron it in place. However, to make sure it remains in position through wear and tear, you do need to press it very well. Place fusible interfacing, glue side down, towards the reverse of the fabric. Cover with a press cloth and hold a hot iron in position for ten seconds. Lift the iron, move it to the next area and press again, without moving the iron around. Once it has been attached firmly, iron all over and then allow the fabric to cool before handling it again. Sew-in interfacing is useful for fabrics that cannot be pressed at high temperatures or prolonged periods such as pile fabrics like fleece, fur or velvet. Sew the interfacing to the wrong side of the main fabric just within the seam allowance and then trim the interfacing close to the stitching to reduce the bulk within the seams.

Waistbanding This is another type of interfacing which is cut to a standard waistband thickness and is usually fusible so it can be ironed in place on the reverse of the fabric. It often has slotted holes along the length which help it fold neatly in half.

Stabilisers These are similar to interfacing and are used to provide support and stability to fabric while it is being sewn, preventing it from distorting, stretching out of shape or puckering. They are usually placed on the reverse of the fabric. There are many kinds available, from the most widely used tear-away variety, to soluble and heat-away versions. You can also use stabilising tape, called stay tape, at neck edges for V or round necks and along shoulder seams. Apply it just within the seam allowance to add support without changing the properties or feel of the fabric.

Double-sided fusible web This usually has a paper backing and is ideal for sticking two fabric layers together prior to stitching. Most frequently used for appliqué, the webbing is ironed on to the reverse of the contrast fabric. A design can then be drawn on the paper backing and cut out. Peel off the paper backing to reveal the second fusible side and iron the appliqué in position on the right side of the main fabric.

Needle threader A real boon when sewing in low light. A very fine wire loop is passed through the eye of the needle, then you insert the thread through the loop and pull the loop and thread back through the needle's eye. This is also useful if you are sewing with thicker threads.

Various types of interfacing, stabilisers, fusible web and waistbanding.

Snap fasteners and self-covered buttons Snap fasteners are a quick alternative to making buttonholes. They are also useful when you want to add another fastening between buttons (such as on a blouse). They come in silver, black and clear plastic in a variety of sizes. Self-covered buttons are ideal for adding a personal and unique finish to cushions, clothing and bags.

Rotary cutter and cutting mat These are very handy for cutting straight edges and shapes very quickly. You can cut layers together too. Use with an acrylic ruler that is easy to hold in place. Slightly angle the cutter so the blade is against the ruler and push it away from you. Good cutting mats are 'self healing' so are not left scored when you cut on them and have handy grids in imperial and/or metric to help you cut to size.

Press cloth Use a press cloth to protect the fabric and work with a hotter iron than the fabric can withstand alone. Cotton organza makes an ideal press cloth as it is transparent and withstands high temperatures.

Fusible hemming tape
A strip of fusible webbing that is placed between fabric layers at the hem to stick them together.

Hooks and eyes
Alternatives to snap fasterners, these metal closures are hand sewn to either side of a gap to hold it together.

Wadding/batting
This is used to pad some of the projects.

Rotary cutter and mat, snap fasteners, needle threader, hooks and eyes, fusible hemming tape, press cloth and pattern paper.

Sewing machine needles

Machine needles come in different sizes to suit different fabric weights. European sizes range from 60–120 and American sizes from 9–20 (see the conversion chart opposite). The lower the number, the finer the needle. Most are marked with both European and American sizing.

The most important needles to have in your workbox are universal/sharps needles for woven fabrics, a jeans needle for thicker fabrics, ballpoint or stretch needles for stretchy knit fabrics and a twin needle for decorative work.

Universal/sharps needles Use to sew woven fabrics. They come in different sizes – lower numbers for finer fabrics, higher numbers for heavyweight. Sharps needles are very fine and suitable for silks and satins and for top stitching and buttonholes.

Jeans needles These are more robust, slightly thicker and have a larger eye for thicker threads. They are best for dense fabric such as denim and furnishing and upholstery fabrics.

Ballpoint or stretch needles These are designed to be used with knitted fabrics. Although it is invisible to the naked eye, they have a slightly rounded tip which parts the fibres rather than piercing them. Using a universal needle on stretch fabric can cause snags, skipped stitches or broken thread.

Twin needles Two needles are attached to the one shank so that you can sew two perfectly parallel rows of stitching at the same time (see page 90). You can get twin needles with different gaps between the needles, from 1.6 for pin tucking to 4.0 for decorative top stitching. They are also available in different weights for lightweight to heavyweight and stretch or universal fabric.

Other useful needles

Embroidery needles These are useful for dense areas of stitching. They have a sharp tip and a larger eye to cope with the rapid and concentrated stitching involved with machine embroidery and appliqué.

Metallic needles Metallic threads produce wonderful results, but they can be shredded if they are stitched with a regular universal needle. Metallic needles have a special coating on the inside of the eye to cope with the metallic thread. Stitch more slowly when working with metallic thread to prevent breakage.

Leather needles These are designed to sew dense fabrics and have a chisel point and shaped shaft to help penetrate fabrics evenly and smoothly. They are also useful for plastics.

Wing needle This has a winged shape either side of the main shaft which is designed to leave little holes in the fabric as you stitch. Wing needles are used for heirloom stitching.

Tip

To remove a needle to replace it, loosen the screw (above the needle to the right) and pull the needle out. You should need to use your screwdriver tool to do this. Insert the new needle as high as it will go, with the flat part of the shank facing the back of the sewing machine. Tighten the screw holding the needle in place by hand and then with the screwdriver to ensure it will not work loose as you sew.

Tips

• Replace your needle after every eight hours of sewing or after every project.

• Use the right needle for the fabric being sewn to prevent holes in the fabric, puckered or snagged fabric or skipped stitches.

• If the thread keeps breaking or you get skipped stitches, check your needle. It could be blunt or bent.

Needle sizes

The different types of needle come in various sizes to suit a variety of fabric weights.
Here is a guide to what size (thickness) needle to use depending on the fabric being sewn.

American	European	Fabric weight
9	60	Fine, lightweight e.g. chiffon, voiles
10	70	Lightweight e.g. organza, silks
11	75	Lingerie, swimwear, fine cottons
12	80	General dressmaking, e.g. cottons, woollens, polyesters, velvets
14	90	Heavier weight woollens, wool crepes, coatings, fleece, soft furnishing cottons
16	100	Heavyweight coatings e.g. dense denim, canvas, heavy brocade
18	110	Heavyweight fabrics, multiple layers, soft furnishing
20	120	Very heavyweight fabrics

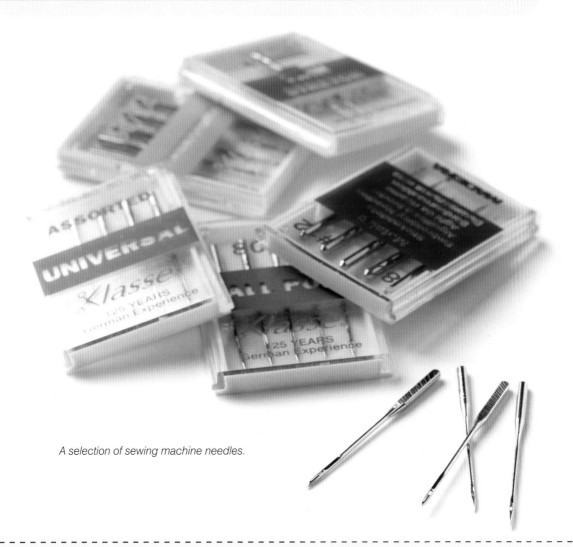

A selection of sewing machine needles.

Fabrics

The right fabric can make all the difference to a project. Sometimes, a beautiful fabric print is all you need to create something with a real 'wow' factor. Which fabric to use depends on whether you want to create something classic and understated or bold and dramatic.

Woven fabrics

Woven fabrics come in a huge varitey of weights, prints and patterns. They have a warp (lengthways threads) and weft (horizontal left to right threads). The side edges are called selvedges, and are neatened, more tightly bound edges. Woven fabrics also have what is known as a grainline. The straight grain runs down the length and is parallel to the selvedge.

Cotton, linen, silk and wool are made from natural fibres, which are often mixed with man-made fibres to create fabrics that are stronger and more crease-resistant.

Common fabric types

- **Cotton:** calico, cheesecloth, muslin, chiffon, voile, organza, tulle, cotton lawn, gingham, linen, damask, drill and denim.
- **Silks:** taffeta, satin, crepe de chine, crepe-back satin, dupion, raw silk, and brocade. Polyester, viscose and rayon are silky man-made alternatives.
- **Wools:** challis, corduroy, angora, alpaca, flannel, gaberdine, wool crepe, boiled wool, bouclé, cashmere, tartan, worsted, tweed, mohair and fleece.

How to sew

Needle and thread: Use general-purpose sewing thread and a needle to suit the fabric thickness – fine universal needles 70–80 (10–12) for lightweight fabric, heavy-duty jeans needles, size 90–110 (14–18) for denim, canvas or multiple layers.

Seams and neatening seams: Stitch seams with straight stitch in a length to suit the fabric weight: 2.2–2.5mm (13) for light to mediumweight fabric and 2.5–3.0 (9) for heavyweight fabrics and multiple layers. Neaten seams with overcast, zigzag stitch or pinking shears. On straight seams, you can also use a French seam (see page 34).

Pressing: Pure cottons and linens can be pressed with a hot iron. For silks, wools and mixed fibre fabrics, always use a press cloth and a medium to hot iron. Press pile fabrics face down on a soft towel to protect the pile of the fabric.

Nap/pile: Check whether there is an obvious pile or nap (surface texture) to the fabric that looks different if brushed one way or the other, as with velvet, fur and some fleece. Always place all pattern pieces in the same direction top to bottom so the pile will lay the same way. Stitch all seams in the direction of the nap whenever possible. Also use 'with nap' layouts for silks and satins as they too can look different when viewed from top to bottom or bottom to top. If your fabric has a one-way pattern or obvious 'right way up,' treat it as a nap fabric and lay all pieces in the same direction from top to bottom.

Tip
Use serrated shears when cutting silks or very fine fabrics. The serrated blades will grip fabric as it is cut.

Tip
Use a walking foot when sewing pile fabrics to help feed both layers evenly. Alternatively, stitch with a wider seam allowance, which also helps feed them more evenly.

Knit fabrics

Knitted fabrics have a definite stretch but no warp or weft threads. They can be light to heavyweight and can be used for close-fitting garments, sportswear and casual wear.

Common fabric types

Cotton jerseys, double knits, Lycra and Spandex, stretch velour and stretch velvet, faux fur and fun fur.

How to sew

Needle and thread: Use ballpoint needles to suit the fabric weight and general purpose thread. Also use woven interfacings that can stretch with the fabric.

Seams and neatening seams: Stay stitch curved seams to prevent them stretching out of shape while you sew. Use stay tape at neck and armholes to prevent unwanted stretch through prolonged wear. For all horizontal seams, use zigzag or stretch stitches that allow the fabric to stretch. While most knit fabrics will not fray, they can curl at the edges, causing visible bumps in the seam if they are left unfinished. To prevent this, neaten with overcast or zigzag stitch or simply stitch a double row of stitching and trim close to the outer row.

Pressing: Use a press cloth to protect the fabric. Press stretch pile fabrics such as velvet face down on a soft towel, to protect the pile of the fabric.

Speciality fabrics

These may be woven or knitted and many have piles and textured surfaces so always use 'with nap' layout. Otherwise treat them as a woven or knitted fabric.

Common fabric types

Faux fur, fun fur, synthetic suede/leather, beaded silks, satins and brocades.

How to sew

Needle and thread: Use a needle to suit the fabric weight. Change needles and pins frequently, particularly when sewing fabrics with metallic fibres. Use silk thread for silks. Use plenty of pins to hold flimsy fabric layers together. For faux leather, avoid pins, which may leave holes. Use tin cans as weights instead.

Seams and neatening seams: Use sew-in interfacings for fabrics with pile or beading. For beaded and sequinned fabrics, use a zipper foot if beading might get in the way. Remove beads from the seam allowance by crushing and gently removing. Cut sequins in half and pull out. On fur fabrics, trim the pile from the seam allowance to reduce bulk. To hide seams in furs, working from the right side, use a pin to pick out the pile from the seam stitching. Cut facings from lining fabric rather than heavy pile fabrics or those with beads and sequins.

Pressing: Always use a press cloth. Avoid pressing fabrics with surface detail such as crushed velvets or pre-pleated fabric. Avoid steam when working with beaded, sequinned or metallic fabrics.

Threads

There is a delicious range of threads available for sewing on a sewing machine nowadays, in a huge selection of colours.

General purpose threads Most general purpose threads are polyester or polyester-covered cottons which have the flexibility of polyester with the strength of cotton. These are fabulous versatile threads, useful for seaming, top stitching and most general sewing projects.

Silk and cotton threads As well as the general purpose threads, there are also pure cotton threads and pure silk threads. Use cottons with cottons, linen and linen-like fabric, and silks with silky fabrics to ensure the thread and fabric have the same wash and wear capabilities. Silk threads are very soft and have a sheen, making them ideal for hand sewing and top stitching.

Machine embroidery Slightly finer than general purpose sewing thread, machine embroidery threads are used for highly concentrated stitching. They often have a high gloss to give the stitching a rich lustre. There is a huge variety available from solid colours to variegated and iridescent. Use a machine embroidery needle when sewing with these threads as it has a larger eye suitable for dense stitching, which will also help prevent the thread splitting or breaking.

Bobbin fill This is a finer thread designed to be used in conjunction with machine embroidery in the bobbin, hence the name. It decreases the density of the stitching on the reverse of the work, which helps prevent puckering. It is most often available in black or white.

Metallic threads These add richness and lustre to even the simplest of stitching and look very glamorous when used with decorative stitching on dark colours. Use a metallic needle which has a coated eye to prevent the metallic fibres from shredding or breaking. Also stitch more slowly. If working with a thicker, uneven metallic thread, wind it on the bobbin and work with the fabric right side down towards the throat plate to ensure the decorative thread is on the right side when finished.

Invisible/transparent Available in clear or smoke colour, this is a nylon thread that looks like fishing line. It is designed for quilting, attaching trims and making invisible repairs. You may need to loosen the tension when using it both in the bobbin and as top thread. Check on a spare piece of fabric first. The stitching will be virtually invisible while creating texture in the surface of the project, which is perfect if you are a little wary of quilting straight lines.

Top stitch/buttonhole thread Buttonhole thread is thicker than standard thread and is meant to be highly visible. It is usually polyester and it can be used for top stitching, decorative stitches or hand sewing buttons. Use a general purpose thread in the bobbin and a jeans needle or machine embroidery needle with a larger eye to accommodate the thicker thread.

Quilting A poly/cotton mix or 100% cotton, quilting thread has a wax finish to help prevent tangling when hand stitching, but it can be used for machine stitching as well.

Basting (tacking) Usually 100% cotton, basting thread is finer and rougher than general thread. It will break easily and is only used for temporarily holding fabrics together.

Hand sewing threads In addition to the machine threads which can be used for hand sewing, there are different, thicker threads used for embroidery, which can also be used with a sewing machine, either on the bobbin, or laid on the top of the fabric and couched in place with a triple zigzag stitch.

Mercerised or perle crochet thread Used for cross stitch or crochet, this is usually 100% cotton and has a slight lustre. You can use this for corded pin tucks or corded buttonholes or couch it on the surface of fabric.

Stranded cotton/embroidery floss This is made up of strands which can be separated and used singly or grouped, depending on the thickness required. Different varieties include high sheen, matt finish, and variegated.

Tip

Match the thread colour to the fabric as closely as possible. When a perfect match is not possible, choose a slightly darker shade as it will be lighter when unravelled from the reel.

WINDING AND FITTING THE BOBBIN

A properly wound bobbin will help create neat, perfect stitching. Use the bobbins provided with your machine and follow our simple steps.

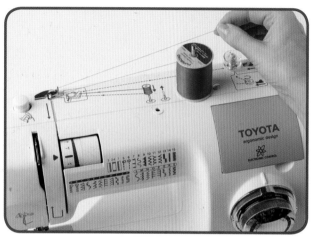

1 Place the thread on the spindle and then follow the marked path to take the thread round the bobbin winding tension on the left and bring it back towards the bobbin.

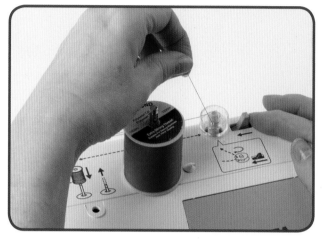

2 Feed the thread end through the hole in the bobbin, from inside to outside, then place the bobbin on the spindle. Push the spindle over, or the lever towards the spindle (depending on your model).

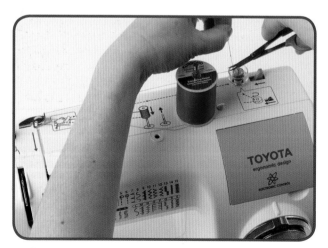

3 Hold the thread tail while you start winding the bobbin. Once a little of the thread is wound round the bobbin, stop winding and cut off the thread tail. Continue to fill bobbin.

Tip

On some machines you need to disengage the needle manually to prevent it going up and down as the bobbin winds. To do this, either pull out a section of the balance wheel or move a lever as shown. Remember to put it back when the bobbin has been wound.

How to fit the bobbin

It is very important that the bobbin is dropped into the bobbin casing correctly even though it looks as if it can go either way up.

1 The thread must come off the bobbin anticlockwise, as shown in the diagram on the bobbin cover.

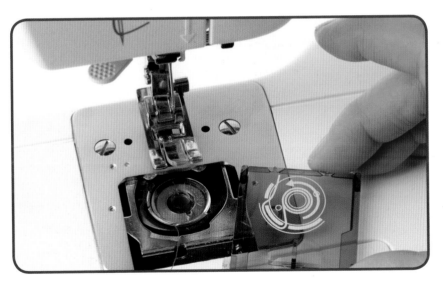

2 Drop the bobbin in place. Take the thread round the little notch and pull it round clockwise, as shown in the diagram.

Tip

Lower and raise the needle to pick up the bobbin thread before replacing the plastic cover, to avoid trapping the thread tail in the cover, which can prevent it being picked up.

Fitting a front-loading bobbin

1 Place the bobbin in the bobbin case with the thread coming off clockwise.

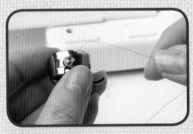

2 Pull the thread through the bobbin tension.

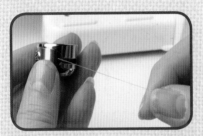

3 Give a little tug on the thread to ensure it is through the tension.

4 Push the bobbin case into place in the machine, matching the arm to the notch hole.

UPPER THREADING

Most machines are threaded in a similar way, following four or five steps. Make sure the needle and presser foot are raised.

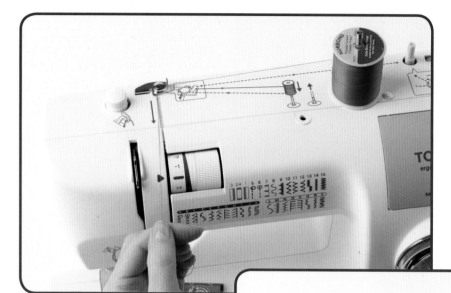

1 Follow the diagram on the top of your machine to begin threading the top thread. Take it round the notch as shown.

2 Take the thread down and round the rectangle marked with an arrow in the direction shown. This takes it through the tension discs.

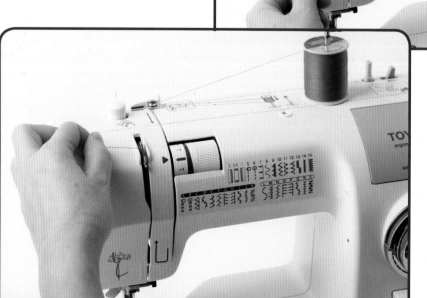

3 Take the thread up to the metal hook, which should be raised and visible. If it is not, turn the balance wheel on the right to raise it. Pull the thread round the hook from right to left and down to the needle.

4 Feed the thread behind the hook above the needle. Lower the presser foot.

5 If you have a needle threader, pull it down fully with your left index finger and hold it down. The threader arm will wrap round the needle.

6 Holding the thread in your right hand, hook it under the left fork of the threader, then under the smaller right fork.

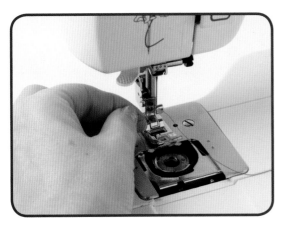

7 Release the threader. There should be a loop of thread coming out of the back of the needle. Pull on the loop.

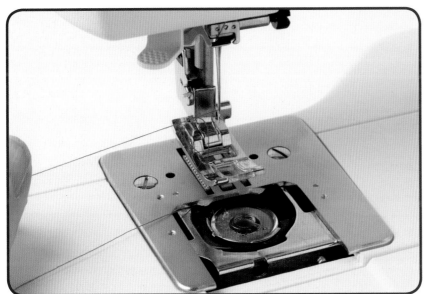

8 To pick up the bobbin thread, turn the balance wheel by hand towards you. This takes the needle down and up again and brings up the bobbin thread. Pull the loop free to pull out the thread end.

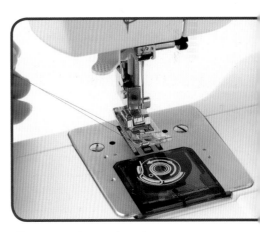

9 Hold both threads to the back and put on the lid to the bobbin compartment.

CHECKING STITCHING AND TENSION

Once you have threaded your machine, test the stitch to ensure it is working perfectly. It is a good idea to do some test stitching every time you change your stitch selection.

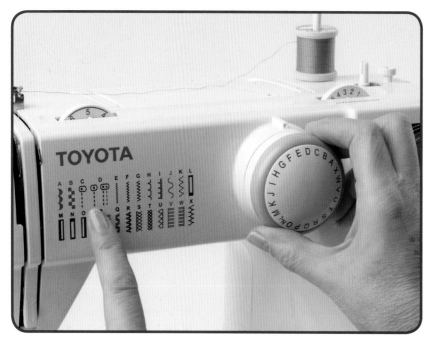

Tip

If something is wrong with the stitching, try rethreading the machine rather than changing the tension as it is more likely to be a problem with the threading.

1 Choose a stitch from the diagrams on your machine and turn the dial to the correct setting.

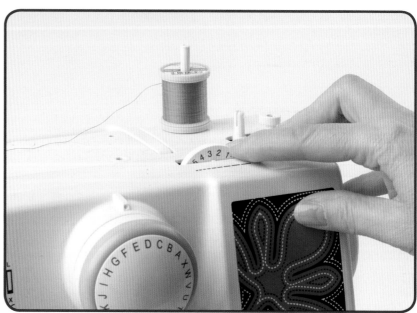

2 Choose a stitch length and turn the dial. For most stitching, 2.2–2.5mm (13 stitches per inch) is a good choice.

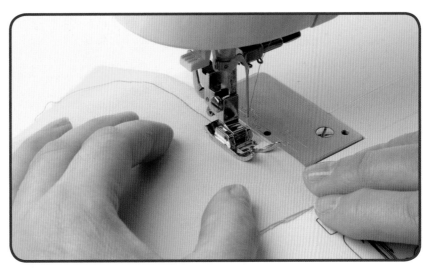

3 It is best to leave the tension setting on your machine alone. On this machine, a line shows on the dial when the machine is set to the right tension for most stitching. Beyond that line in either direction, you are loosening or tightening the tension.

4 Place the fabric under the presser foot, using the right edge or the markings on the throat plate as a guide. These markings denote the distance from the needle when it is in its automatic default position. Arrange your fabric accordingly. Hold the threads at the rear, put the presser food down and turn the balance wheel to put the needle down. Holding the thread tails in your left hand, start stitching. Guide the fabric through with both hands, neither pulling nor pushing it.

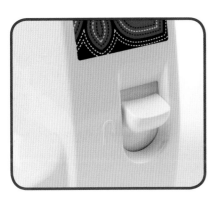

5 To reverse the direction of the stitching, to secure a seam, push down the reverse button (pictured), hold it down and go back two or three stitches. Release the button and continue forwards as required.

6 To finish a line of stitching, turn the balance wheel by hand to raise the needle, raise the presser foot, pull out the fabric and trim the thread ends very close to the stitching.

The stitching on the left has come out wrong. This could mean that the machine was not threaded properly, or that the bobbin is the the wrong way up.

This shows the stitching as it should come out: the top pink thread on the top of the fabric and the yellow bobbin thread showing on the back.

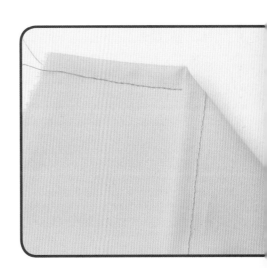

TRYING OUT YOUR MACHINE'S STITCHES

A very good way to get to know your machine is to try out the stitches provided. Take a couple of hours to play, stitching out the stitches as they are and then changing length and width if your machine has stitch length and width dials. Make a sampler and note on it the stitches used, and any changes you have made so that you can quickly recreate these options later. Remember to raise the needle every time you change your stitch choice as it will move from side to side.

Basic stitches

These are the basic stitches that will be found on most sewing machines. More advanced machines will have lots of additional decorative stitches.

Straight stitch

Used for seaming and top stitching. There may be one or two options for straight stitch: changing the needle position from centre to left (or right) and/ or two stitch lengths.

Blind hem stitch

Used to hem projects invisibly, this has either a straight stitch with single zigzag repeated along the line, or a small zigzag with one larger zigzag repeated along the line. The zigzag option is for stretch fabrics but can be used on woven fabrics too.

Overcast/overedge stitch

A straight line of stitches with repeated zigzag to the right. Use an overcast foot to stitch this on the very edge of the fabric to neaten raw edges. It also makes a nice decorative stitch.

Buttonhole stitch

This may be a single stitch, so the buttonhole is sewn in one pass, or a four-step buttonhole where you have step 1 for the left arm of the buttonhole, step 2 to stitch one end bar tack, step 3 for the right arm of the buttonhole and then step 4 (same as step 2) for the final bar tack. You will also need to reduce the stitch length to absolute minimum (almost 0). Note that the markings on the stitch length dial will colour-correspond or have a buttonhole image.

Zigzag stitch/ triple zigzag stitch

A row of stitches that are worked side to side as you stitch. If you have the option to change length and width, you can make these closer together (by reducing the stitch length) and alter how wide they are from side to side by increasing or decreasing the stitch width. A triple zigzag stitch is made up of three little stitches as it goes from side to side. This is a good stitch for stretch fabrics and also for holding down ribbons or thick threads laid on the surface of a fabric.

Stretch stitch

This is a small, slanted zigzag stitch used to sew seams on stretchy fabric so that the stitching will stretch with the fabric.

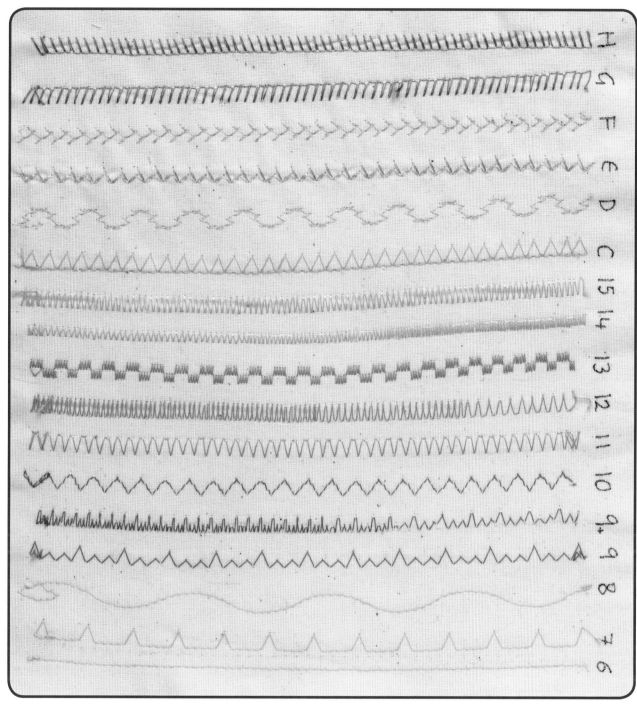

A test sampler showing the stitches available on one machine with their letters or numbers shown on the right.

USING YOUR MACHINE

STRAIGHT STITCH

Straight stitching is used for so many aspects of sewing projects – from simple seaming to attaching pockets or trims and hemming. Straight stitching is quite simply a row of stitches in a single line.

Straight stitch seam

This is the most commonly used seam for woven fabrics. The stitch length depends on the fabric thickness and the number of layers being sewn together. For lightweight fabrics, use between 2–2.5mm (13 stitches per inch), for mediumweight fabric 2.5–3mm (9 stitches per inch) and for heavyweight fabrics between 3–4mm (9–6 stitches per inch). With the fabric layers right sides together, stitch down the seam line, leaving a seam allowance to the right of the needle of between 6–15mm ($\frac{1}{4}$ –$\frac{5}{8}$in) depending on the project.

Use the stitching guidelines on the throat plate – most are marked in 3mm ($\frac{1}{8}$in) increments – or the edge of the presser foot, or use masking tape to mark your own guide positioned the distance from the needle that you require. On close-fitting garments or patchwork projects, mark the stitching line with a chalk pencil to ensure total accuracy.

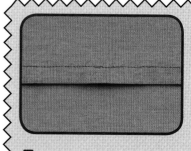

Tip

Avoid threads tangling at the start of a seam by holding both bobbin and top thread tails behind the needle.

French seam

Stitch with the wrong sides of the fabric together, taking a 6mm ($\frac{1}{4}$in) seam allowance. Trim the seam allowance to 3mm ($\frac{1}{8}$in) and then turn the fabric right sides together with the seam on the edge. Press and stitch again 1cm ($\frac{3}{8}$in) from the edge, encasing the trimmed seam allowance neatly.

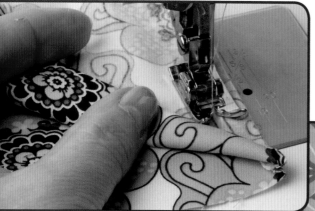

Bias seam

Fabric cut on the bias has more stretch and needs to be treated slightly differently and with care. To avoid seams rippling, slightly stretch the fabric in front and behind the needle as you sew. Carefully press, using a press cloth to relax the the stitching into a smooth seam. On heavyweight fabrics, add a strip of interfacing or stay tape to the bias seam line to prevent the fabrics from drooping and sagging later.

Double stitched seam

Stitch the first row along the seam line as usual, using a straight stitch, then stitch the second row a scant 3mm ($\frac{1}{8}$in) away, stitching in the same direction, using either a straight or small zigzag stitch. Trim close to the outer stitching. These seams are used to stitch and neaten sheer fabrics or laces and to help prevent the fabric curling on stretch fabrics.

Top stitching

This is stitching that is purposefully visible on the right side of the fabric. Top stitching can be used to hold facings or hems in place too. It helps make the seam more durable as well as providing a crisp edge. Use a thread colour to match fabric if it is a purely functional stitch, but use contrast thread and colour for a bold statement.

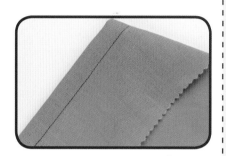

Edge stitching

This is the same as top stitching, but created close to the edge. It is used to attach patch pockets or trims and is generally worked in a thread colour to match the attachment so it is virtually invisible.

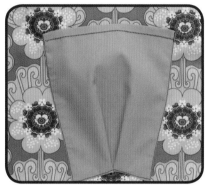

Edge stitching shown on the outer edges of a pocket.

Stay stitching

This is used to prevent unwanted stretching while you are handling fabrics. It is a line of straight stitching at regular stitch length to suit the fabric, just within the seam allowance. Use it on areas cut on the bias such as round or V-necklines and around armholes. NB: You can also get iron-on stay-stitching tape which can be fused in place along the seamline.

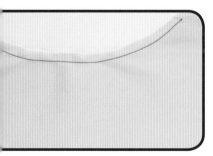

DRAWSTRING BAGS

Get to grips with your new machine by making some handy drawstring bags.

Finished sizes

Small – 14 x 14cm (5½ x 5½in)
Medium – 25 x 25cm (10 x 10in)
Large – 46 x 33cm (18 x 13in)

You will need

Small bag: 38 x 16cm (15 x 6¼in) rectangle of printed cotton

Medium bag: 60 x 27cm (23½ x 10½in) rectangle of printed cotton

Large bag: 102 x 35cm (40 x 13¾in) rectangle of printed cotton

Ruler

Water soluble pen

Iron

1–1.50m (1–1½ yd) of wide contrasting cord or thin ribbon

Matching sewing thread

Pinking shears

Large safety pin

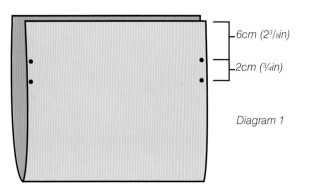

6cm (2³/₈in)

2cm (¾in)

Diagram 1

1 Fold the fabric panel in half, right sides together and with the fold at the bottom. Mark the casing opening at the side seams by measuring down from the top edge on either side by 6cm (2³/₈in) and making a mark with a washable pen. Measure down another 2cm (¾in) to leave room for the casing and mark the seam. See Diagram 1 above.

2 Taking a 1cm (³/₈in) seam allowance, stitch the side seams from the top to the first mark. Reverse stitch to secure the stitching. Start again at the second mark, leaving the casing section unstitched. Again reverse stitch at the start of the seam to secure the stitching, then continue to the bottom of the bag. Repeat for the other side seam. Trim the seam allowance with pinking shears and press the seams open.

3 Still with the bag wrong side out, create a gusseted bottom by refolding the bag so the side seams lay on top of the bottom fold to create triangles at the bottom side edges (see Diagram 2). Stitch across the triangle about 3cm (1¼in) from the tip. Trim the excess triangles off using pinking shears (see inset). Press.

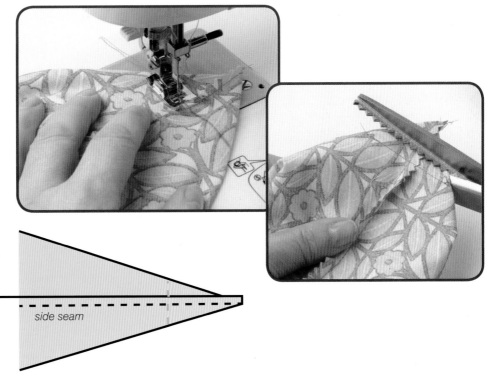

Diagram 2

side seam

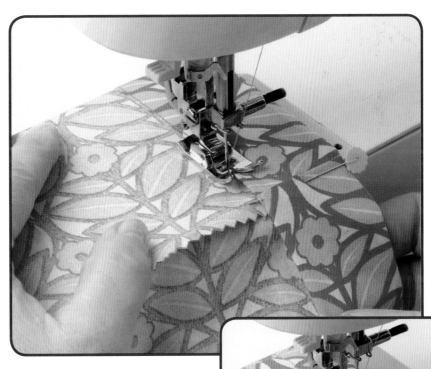

4 To make the casing, turn under the top end by 5cm (2in), tucking under the raw edge by 1cm (³⁄₈in), and press. Stitch all the way round close to the turned-under fold (which should be just below the open seam at the side edges). Stitch a parallel row of stitches 2cm (¾in) above the first row (see inset).

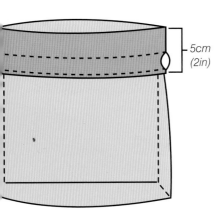

5cm
(2in)

Diagram 3

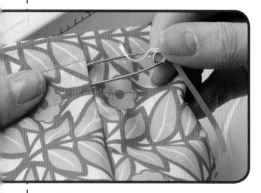

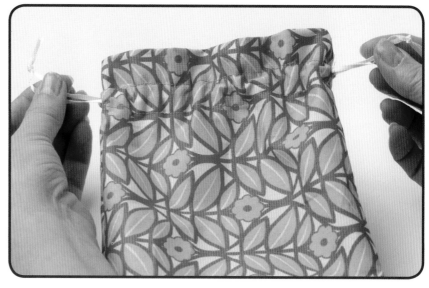

5 Cut the ribbon or cord into two equal lengths. Using a safety pin, feed one end of one length through the casing all the way round and come out the same side.

6 Knot the ends together. Feed the second piece through from the other side edge, again all the way round, then knot the ends together.

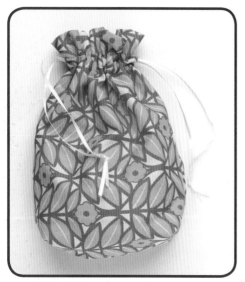

The finished drawstring bag.

Opposite and below

A variety of drawstring bags made using the same techniques. To add a pocket, see the Tip below.

Tip

Add a contrasting pocket to the bag front before stitching the side seams. Cut a rectangle 14 x 12cm (5½ x 4¾in). Turn under 1cm (³/₈in) all the way round and press. Machine stitch across one long edge (which will be the pocket opening). Position the pocket on the bag front and machine stitch in place along the side and bottom edges.

ZIGZAG STITCH

A zigzag stitch is a basic sewing stitch with sideways width but it can also be altered to create other stitches such as satin stitch. It can be used to sew seams, attach trims, neaten or cover raw edges or simply as a decorative stitch.

Zigzag foot

This is usually the foot that is already attached to the sewing machine. It has a large aperture through which the needle can go to the left and the right as it forms the zigzag stitch. This foot is also used if you wish to move the needle position to the left or right (if your machine has that capability) so that it can still go through the foot without hitting the sides. The foot will also have a slightly indented channel on the underside which will help it glide smoothly over concentrated stitching.

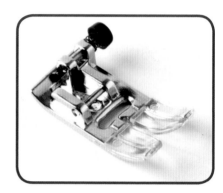

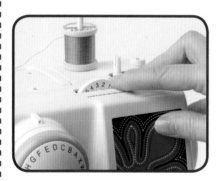

Selecting and altering the stitch

Your machine may have one or two widths of zigzag stitch and a stretch stitch (which looks like a tiny slanted zigzag). Select the stitch, making sure the needle is raised as you do so as it will move from side to side.
If your machine has stitch length and width dials you can alter the zigzag stitch to create narrower stitching for seams, or as a decorative finish. Decreasing the stitch length will bring the stitches close together. The stitch width alters how wide they are from side to side.

Seams

Use a small zigzag stitch or a stretch stitch when sewing seams on knit fabrics that need to stretch after they are stitched. If you can adjust the length and width, reduce the length to 1–1.5mm (24) and width to 2.5mm for lightweight fabrics and set the length to 2–2.5mm (13) and the width at 2–3mm for heavier weight fabrics.

Tip
Some areas of knit fabrics need to have the stretch minimised, such as shoulder seams and necklines. Stitch these with a straight stitch.

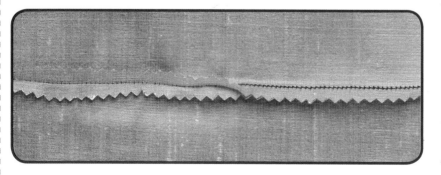

A zigzag stitch seam on a stretch fabric.

Neatening edes and seams

Neaten the raw edges of fabrics using a zigzag stitch on woven fabric so the right swing of the stitch is just off the fabric edge. If you have an overcast/overedge foot, use it for stitching on the edge of fabric as it holds the fabric flat as you stitch. Lightweight fabrics can have both seam allowances neatened together as one. On heavier weight fabrics, press seam allowances open and neaten separately (see below).

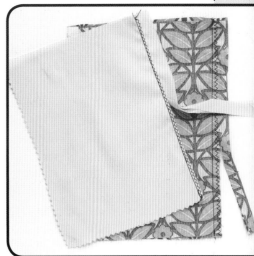

To neaten knit fabrics, stitch the zigzag stitch on the seam allowance close to the seam and then trim the excess seam allowance close to the stitching (see above right).

Triple zigzag stitch

This stitch creates the zigzag stitch with three tiny stitches going each way. It is useful for attaching elastic or trims to a fabric as it catches them down in place. Adjust the width so that it stitches just over the edges on either side as well as through the middle.

Satin stitch and appliqué

This is a particularly useful stitch to cover the edges of appliqué. Decrease the stitch length to a very short 0.3mm or 0.5mm (60) so that stitches are formed very close together. Decrease the width if desired to make a narrow satin stitch or leave it wider for stitching letter shapes.

Moving the needle

On most modern machines the stitch width dial can be used to move the needle position, which is very useful if you wish to stitch closer to the edge of the fabric. Use the presser foot edge as a guide for the fabric edge, move the needle to the far right and you can edge stitch easily. To move the needle, select straight stitch and then use the stitch width dial to move the needle to the left, centre or right. Note that how far you can move the needle depends on your make and model. Basic machines will not have this option but instead may have two or three straight stitch choices for stitching further left, centre or right.

Appliqué

Appliqué is the term used for sewing one or more fabric shapes on the surface of a base fabric. The appliqué can be a motif, a shape such as flower or even letters cut from fabric.

Making an appliqué

The easiest method is to iron a piece of paper-backed double-sided fusible web to the reverse of the appliqué fabric. Draw a design on the paper backing and then cut out the appliqué. Peel off the paper backing to reveal the other glue surface of the webbing and position the appliqué on the right side of the base fabric, glue side down.

Press the appliqué in place with a hot iron, using a press cloth to protect your fabric.

The raw edges of the appliqué now need to be covered with stitching to prevent them fraying.

Satin stitch

A quick way to cover the fabric edges is to use a zigzag stitch which has been altered to a satin stitch. Select the zigzag stitch and then alter the stitch length to a scant 0.3–0.9mm (60 stitches per inch), depending on the thickness of the fabric layers. Reduce the stitch width to 3. Try the stitch on a sample of fabric with the same number of layers as your project. Position the project under the presser foot so that the needle will swing from just inside the appliqué on the left on to the main base fabric on the right as you stitch. At outer curves, stop with the needle down in the base fabric, raise the presser foot and slightly pivot the fabric so that you continue to cover the raw edge of the appliqué as you sew round the shape.

Blanket stitch

Another stitch option to neaten appliqué is blanket stitch. This has a straight stitch with repeated straight stitches to the left. As it does not completely cover the fabric edge of the appliqué, either turn under the edges of the appliqué fabric before fusing it in place, or use a fabric that does not fray easily. Stitch so the straight line of stitching goes along the edge of the appliqué and the left swing of the stitch is on the appliqué.

Raw edge appliqué

This is another, fast and fun appliqué technique. The raw edges of the applied fabric are left unstitched and are meant to fray a little. Simply attach the appliqué with straight stitch in any design chosen – such as our yellow flower, which is made from layers of petals cut from a lightweight cotton.

Opposite

The flowers show both raw-edge appliqué (left) and satin stitched appliqué (right). The flower pot has edges turned under and stitched in place with a machine appliqué/blanket stitch edging and other decorative stitching along the top.

HEART-FELT APPLIQUÉ PILLOW

Make a special pillow for the bedroom or a loved one and add simple appliqué using zigzag stitch.

Finished size

50 x 40cm (19¾ x 15¾in)

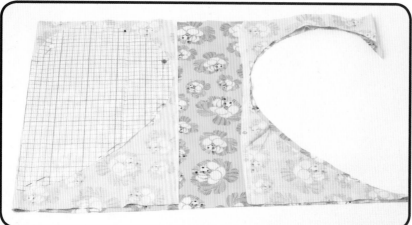

You will need

50cm (½yd) of 110cm (44in) wide cotton fabric

20 x 25cm (8 x 10in) of appliqué (coordinating) fabric

40cm (15¾in) of wadding/batting

Bag of polyester stuffing

Thread to match main and appliqué fabrics

Paper-backed fusible web

Paper and pencil

1 Draw a large half heart shape on paper to create a template. Make the half heart 40cm (15¾in) high and 25cm (10in) wide, starting at the fold. Fold the selvedge edges of the main fabric in towards the centre as shown, right sides together. Pin the half heart template to one fold of the fabric. Cut out a heart. Flip the template over and repeat on the other fold to cut out a second heart.

2 Use the template to cut one complete heart from wadding.

3 Fuse a 20 x 25cm (8 x 10in) piece of paper-backed fusible web to the wrong side of the appliqué fabric. Once cool, fold the fabric in half, right sides together and draw a half heart on the fusible web paper backing, starting at the fold so that you get a perfectly symmetrical shape. Draw the half heart approximately 18cm high and 12cm wide (7 x 4¾in). Cut it out and unfold it.

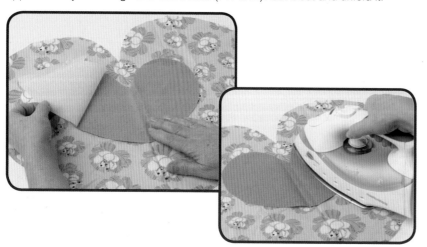

4 Place the heart on the right side of one of the main pillow pieces. Once you are happy with the position, peel off the paper backing and fuse the heart in place using a hot iron (protect more fragile fabrics with a press cloth).

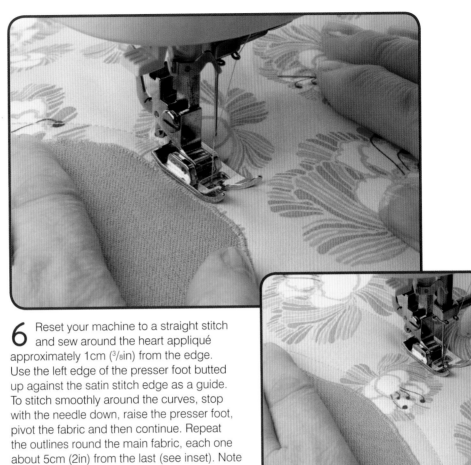

5 Pin the wadding to the wrong side of the main fabric heart. Set the machine to zigzag stitch and decrease the stitch length to 0.03mm (60) so that it closes up the zigzag to create a 'satin stitch'. Try out the stitch on scrap fabric first. Stitch the appliqué heart in place through all the layers. Stitch with the right swing of the needle on the main fabric and the left swing on the appliqué fabric. At curves, stop with the needle down in the main fabric, raise the presser foot and pivot the fabric a little. Lower the presser foot and continue. Repeat this action to stitch smoothly around the heart shape.

6 Reset your machine to a straight stitch and sew around the heart appliqué approximately 1cm (³/₈in) from the edge. Use the left edge of the presser foot butted up against the satin stitch edge as a guide. To stitch smoothly around the curves, stop with the needle down, raise the presser foot, pivot the fabric and then continue. Repeat the outlines round the main fabric, each one about 5cm (2in) from the last (see inset). Note that the third and fourth outlines will not go all round the heart.

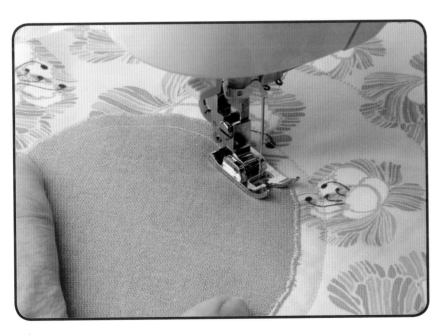

7 Stitch a final outline inside the appliqué about 13mm (½in) from the edge. Use the presser foot edge as a guide along the satin stitch as before, with the foot aligned to the right edge of the satin stitch.

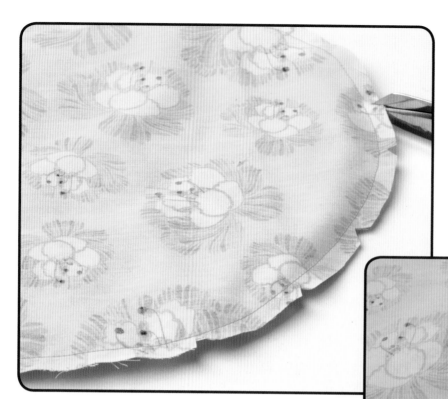

8 Pin the pillow front to the pillow back with right sides together and, taking a 15mm ($^5/_8$in) seam allowance, stitch round the outside edges, leaving a turning gap of approximately 18cm (7in) in one side. Trim the seam allowance, clipping into it at angles to help it lay flat when turned through. At the centre of the heart top, snip close to but not through the stitching (see inset photograph). Leave the unstitched seam allowance at the gap untrimmed so it is easier to sew up later.

9 Turn the pillow right sides out and press it. Fill it with polyester stuffing until it is nicely rounded out. Slip stitch the opening closed.

The finished Heart Felt Appliqué Pillow and (left) a detail.

BUTTONHOLES

Many people shy away from making buttonholes but on today's modern machines, they really are a breeze – whether you have a one, three or more step buttonhole function on your machine – as long as the main ingredients are right. These include the correct combination of fabric, stabiliser and thread, plus a sharp needle.

Some machines have just one type of buttonhole – which is the general rectangle, while others have a variety including knit fabric buttonholes, keyhole buttonholes (for heavy winter wear and coats) and more. All are stitched in the same fashion.

Fabric choice

All fabrics can have buttonholes successfully sewn on them, even if they are lightweight voiles or stretchy knits. The way to succeed is to stabilise the area with appropriate interfacing or stabiliser. This prevents the fabric puckering or being pulled into the feed dogs.

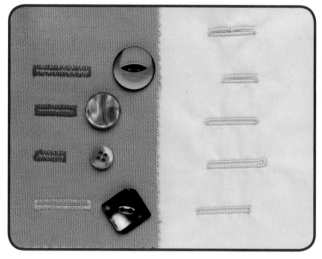

A variety of buttonholes and buttons.

Thread

A good general purpose sewing thread is perfect. It is essential that the same thread is used in the bobbin and on top as the threads show on both sides. If you want to make a feature of the buttonhole, you can use buttonhole thread (on heavyweight garments) or silk thread on silky garments.

Interfacing/stabiliser

All buttonholes should have some sort of stabiliser included. This can be interfacing to add stability, or waistbanding, tear-away or soluble stabiliser. This is because concentrated stitching can cause the fabric to pucker if it is not strengthened. The interfacing helps prevent puckering or pulling and keeps the area stable when buttoned up. If sewing transparent fabrics, use a soluble stabiliser that can be washed away once the buttonhole is stitched. This will help prevent the fabric from bunching and puckering or even being pulled down into the feed dogs.

Needle

Use a new needle appropriate for the fabric (sharps for woven fabric, ballpoint for knits), as buttonholes are made with lots of little zigzag stitches (satin stitch) worked closely together, thus lots of penetration through three or more layers.

Making buttonholes

1 Interface or stabilise the buttonhole area by applying fusible interfacing to the wrong side of the fabric. Allow it to cool completely before continuing. When sewing transparent fabrics, only interface the small area of each buttonhole, adding an extra layer of tear-away stabiliser under the fabric.

Measuring and marking

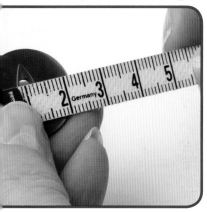

2 If working without a pattern, determine the size of the buttonhole by measuring across the button, then add 3mm (1/8in). For domed or novelty buttons, measure all the way round the button, halve the measurement and add the 3mm (1/8in). Test on a sample first.

3 For vertical buttonholes (such as for blouses or bag closures), mark the buttonhole positions at least 2cm (3/4in) from the fabric edge. If stitching a row of vertical buttonholes, chalk a centre line from top to bottom of the buttonhole area then mark each buttonhole length, at right angles to the centre line, spacing each approximately 6–8cm (2³/₈–3in) apart. It is a good idea to use a different colour chalk for the top and bottom of the buttonhole so you can easily see which is a buttonhole and which is a space between (see above, left). Buttonholes on lightweight fabric are closer, on soft furnishings the gap can be 10–13cm (4–5in).

For horizontal buttons, chalk or thread baste two parallel lines the width of the buttonhole apart, from top to bottom of the buttonhole area. Evenly space the buttonhole positions along the marked lines, like the rungs of a ladder. Place them 6–8cm (2³/₈–3in) apart for garments, 10–13cm (4–5in) apart for soft furnishings. If you are using commercial patterns, simply transfer the buttonhole markings from the tissue to the right side of the fabric.

Stitching a one-step buttonhole

Some machines will have a one-step buttonhole. Simply select the stitch, ensure the stitch length is right down to almost 0 and place the fabric under the foot. It will stitch the entire buttonhole in one pass.

Stitching a four-step buttonhole

On other machines there are four steps to a buttonhole: down the left side, a bar tack at the end, up the right side and a bar tack at the top end. Check your user's manual to determine the type of buttonhole function you have and test it on a scrap of the same fabric with interfacing.

Tip

Make sure the needle is raised before changing the dial as the needle will move each time.

1 The buttonhole foot will have markings down the left-hand side and a tiny hook at the top with little forks at the front.

2 You may need to alter the stitch length – most machines have the optimum length marked in the same colour as the buttonhole stitch selector. The closer to 0 you go, the tighter together the stitches will be. Depending on your fabric choice, you can stitch with the length at almost 0 (60 stitches per inch) or up to 1 (24 stitches per inch).

3 Choose the first part of the buttonhole by selecting the stitch with the left side stitched. Starting at the end of the buttonhole marked on the fabric, stitch up to the far end and stop with the needle raised.

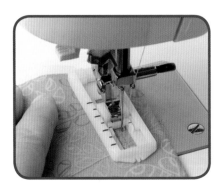

4 Change to the bar tack stitch of the buttonhole sequence and stitch four or five stitches across the end.

5 Change the stitch selection again, to the right side of the buttonhole sequence and stitch back to the beginning, stopping with the needle raised.

6 Change stitch selection to the bar tack again and stitch four to five stitches at the top end of the buttonhole. Finish by taking the thread tails through to the back and feeding them through the stitching before cutting them off.

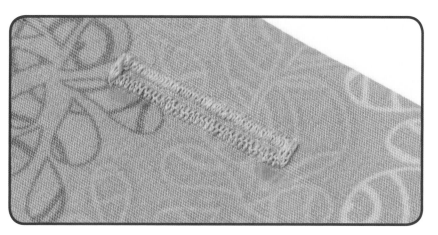

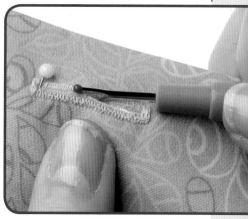

The completed buttonhole stitching. This sample shows the difference between a short stitch length (top long edge) and a longer one (bottom long edge).

7 To open the buttonhole, place a pin at one end just inside the bar tack, then using the seam ripper, start at the other end and push the seam ripper towards the pin. The pin prevents the seam ripper from cutting into the bar tacks at the end of the buttonhole. If necessary, trim off any stray fabric threads inside the opening.

Stitching a corded buttonhole

A corded buttonhole is more robust and will stand proud of the fabric. Use a corded buttonhole on stretch fabrics to help them maintain their shape or on heavier fabrics on which you want a more prominent buttonhole.

1 Hook the cord you are using, in this case crochet cotton, over the tiny hook at the top of the buttonhole foot, and pull the ends through the notch at the bottom. Fit the foot on the machine.

2 Continue with the stages of buttonhole sewing shown opposite. The machine will stitch over the two cords as though couching them down, to create reinforced borders for the buttonhole. When the stitches are complete, pull the ends of the cord so that the loop is concealed at the end of the buttonhole.

A button used to good effect to fasten and finish a clutch bag. Instructions for making the bag begin on page 52.

PARTY CLUTCH BAG

This gorgeous clutch bag is perfect for an evening out. It has a really retro feel and is simple to make.

Finished size:

28cm (11in) wide, 14cm (5½in) high, 5cm (2in) deep.

You will need

Fat quarter (56 x 50cm/18 x 22in) of printed cotton for main fabric

Fat quarter of plain cotton for lining

60 x 48cm (24 x 19in) of heavyweight interfacing

Pale lime green thread

Large decorative button

1 Cut out the bag pieces in the main fabric and the lining fabric as follows: front 30 x 16cm (12 x 6¼in); back and flap (one section) 30 x 32cm (12 x 12½in).

2 Cut out interfacing for all the pieces, (main and lining). Fuse interfacing to the wrong side of each fabric piece.

3 Pin and tack the bag front to the bag back, with the bottom edges matching and the right sides together. Stitch the side seams and bottom.

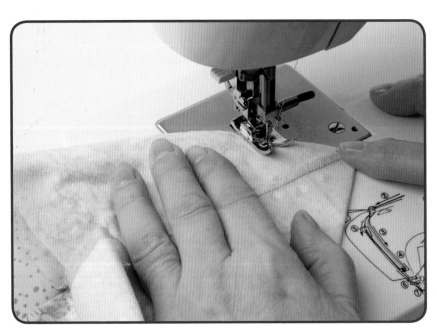

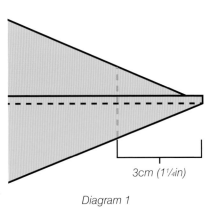

3cm (1¼in)

Diagram 1

4 Create the gusset at the bottom by folding the bottom corners flat, with the side seam laying on top of the bottom seam. Measure 3cm (1¼in) from the point and draw a straight line across to create a triangle (see Diagram 1). Stitch twice along this line and then trim away the excess. Turn the bag right sides out and press.

5 To make the lining, stitch the front to the back as for the bag, but leave a gap of approximately 18cm (7in) in the bottom seam for turning through. Leave inside out.

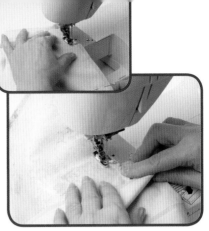

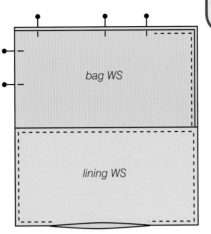

6 Place the main bag inside the lining, right sides together, matching the side seams. Pin in place.

bag WS

lining WS

Diagram 2

7 Stitch across the top edge of the bag front (inset). Stitch round the flap, matching up with the existing seam. See Diagram 2.

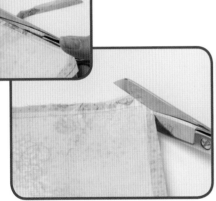

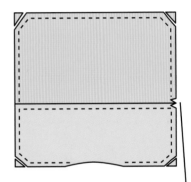

8 Trim the seam allowances (inset) and snip the corners across at an angle. Snip into the seam allowance where the bag front joins the flap (see photograph, above right, and Diagram 3, right). Turn the bag out through the gap in the lining and slip stitch the lining closed.

Diagram 3

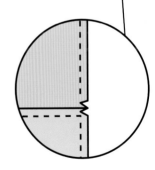

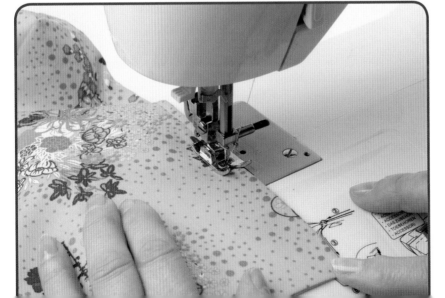

9 Top stitch close to the edge around the flap and across the front of the bag.

10 Make a vertical buttonhole in the centre of the flap approximately 2.5cm (1in) from the bottom edge. Stitch the button on the bag front in the corresponding place.

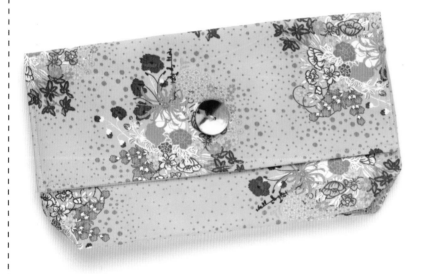

The finished Party Clutch Bag.

ZIPS AND PIPING

Two of the most common types of zip insertion are centred and lapped. Centred zips are used in the back seams of dresses or in trousers and in soft furnishings such as cushion covers. Lapped zips are used in the side seams of dresses, trousers and skirts when the zip is on the left side of the garment.

Use the zipper foot to insert zips. These are frequently part of the sewing machine tool kit and usually have one solid section with indents and a bar to fix the foot to the holder either side. Attach the foot so that this sits to the right of the stitching line when sewing the right side of a zip and to the left when sewing the left side.

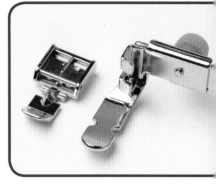

Zipper feet. The one on the right can be moved right or left along the bar to get closer to piping or zip teeth.

How to put in a centred zip

This is a quick method of inserting a centred zip with minimal hand stitching.

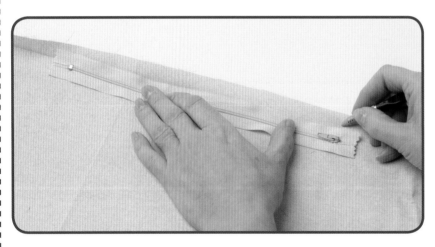

1 Mark the length and position of the zip opening with a pin or chalk pencil on the reverse of your fabric. If you are using a paper pattern, the zip position will be on the tissue piece, so simply transfer the markings to the wrong side of your fabric.

2 Stitch the seam up to the first mark, then cut the thread. Increase the stitch length on your machine to the longest and, starting 5cm (2in) further on, stitch with a long basting stitch, which will be removed later, to the second mark. Change the stitch length back to the normal setting of 2.2–2.5mm (13) and finish the seam.

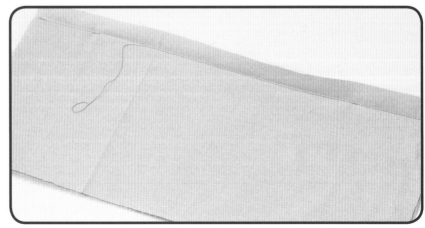

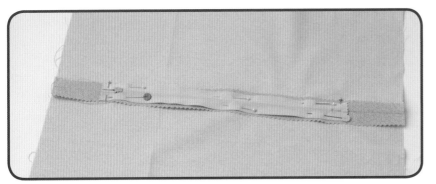

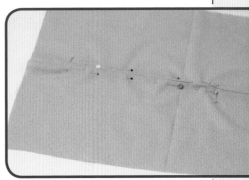

3 Open up the seam and press it flat. Neaten the raw edges. Lay the zip face down with the zip pull over the opening left in step 2. Pin the zip in place from the reverse side, across the bottom and up the sides. Pin in a nice straight line on the zip tape.

4 Turn the piece over and pin the zip in place from the right side. You can now take the first pins out.

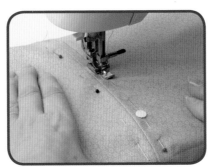

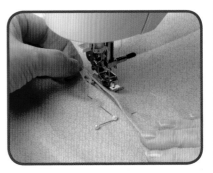

5 Put the zipper foot on the machine. Start at the centre seam at the end of the zip and at right angles to it. The needle should be on the left of the foot.

6 Stitch four stitches across, and then stop with the needle down, raise the presser foot to pivot and stitch up the side of the seam, following the pins.

7 Stop stitching when close to the zip pull, raise the presser foot with the needle down and ease the zip pull below the foot. Continue to the top.

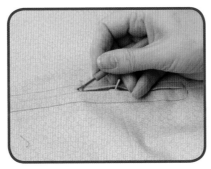

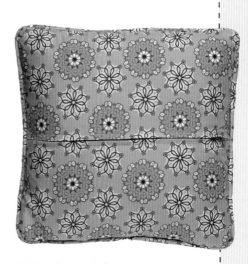

8 Start again at the bottom and stitch the second side. This time the needle should be on the right of the foot.

9 Unpick the basting stitch with a seam ripper.

A finished centred zip.

How to put in a lapped zip

A lapped zip has one flap with just one row of stitching on view. The lap covers the zip teeth, while the other side is stitched very close to the teeth.

1 Mark the zip position and baste (tack) the zip seam together. Machine stitch the rest of the seam, down to the hem as before (see page 56).

2 With the zip open and face down, pin then baste the zip tape to the left-hand seam allowance only, with the teeth of the zip along the seam.

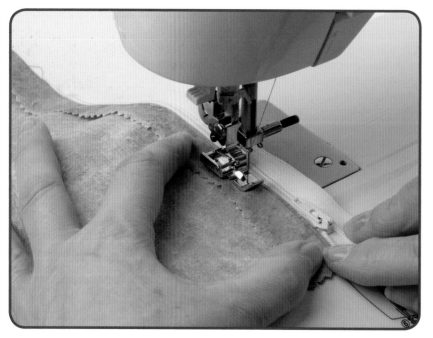

3 Close the zip and fold the seam allowance along the zip teeth so the tiniest amount of seam allowance is visible. Using a zipper foot, machine as close to the teeth as possible along this tiny part of the left seam allowance. The needle should be on the side of the zipper foot closest to the zip.

4 Snip into the seam allowance below the zip end.

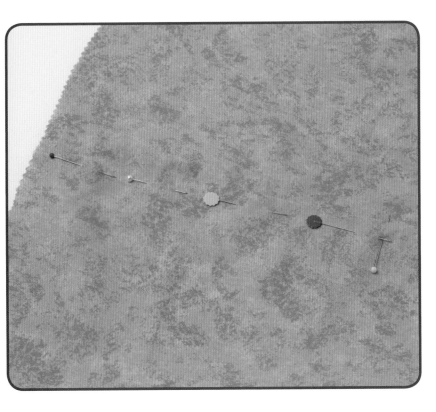

5 Working on a flat surface, place the garment right side down and ensure the zip lies flat and evenly. Then pin the right side of the zip tape through all thickness across the bottom and up the side, 6mm (¼in) from the centre of the teeth. Turn the work over to the right side and repin from the top. Remove the pins on the wrong side.

6 Working from the right side, follow the pins and machine stitch across the bottom and up to the top (see page 57), between 6–12mm (¼–½in) from the teeth. The distance depends on the thickness of the fabric: finer fabrics can be stitched closer, but woollens and fleece should be stitched a little further away. Remove the basting (tacking) stitches with a seam ripper and the zip is complete.

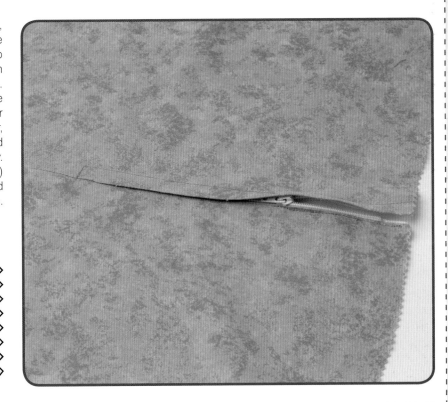

Tip

To ensure a straight line, draw a chalk line along the stitching line or place a piece of masking tape to guide you.

Piping

Piping defines the edge of a seam on a garment or the edges of cushions and seat pads and makes a simple project look professionally finished. You can buy flange piping that already has the rolled edge and tape, or you can make your own by using fabric to encase fine cord for lightweight fabrics or fashions, or a chunky cord for soft furnishings.

To make your own piping you will need to cut strips of fabric on the bias (at a 45° angle to the selvedge) so that it has some stretch in it and can be sewn around curves smoothly. To find the bias, fold the cut edge of the fabric up to the selvedge. The fold is on the bias.

Making your own piping

1 Cut bias strips 5cm (2in) wide, which will be joined to get a total length of the seams to be piped. As a guide, on a 40cm (15¾in) cushion, you will need about 160cm (63in) plus 10cm (4in) for going around the corners and overlapping the ends.

> ### Note
> We have made a small, circular pincushion but the method is the same for a standard cushion. The quantities given are for a standard cushion.

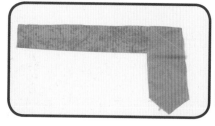 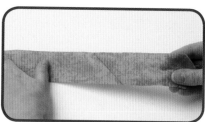

2 To create one long piece of piping fabric from your cut lengths, you will need to join the shorts ends. To maintain the stretch in the fabric, do this by placing the ends at right angles to each other, right sides together. Stitch from the top left corner to the bottom right corner. Trim off the excess.

3 Fold the piping strip in half lengthways, wrong sides together and press. At one short end, tuck the raw edge inside and press. Sandwich piping cord within the strip, pushing it close to the fold. Machine stitch down the strip to hold the cord in place.

Attaching the piping to a cushion cover

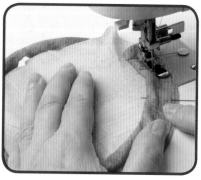

4 Pin the piping to the front of the cushion cover, right sides together, matching raw edges, starting with the end that has been tucked inside the strip. Fit the zipper foot on the machine and set the needle to the left of the foot. Begin stitching 4cm (1½in) from the beginning, stitching close to the piping cord.

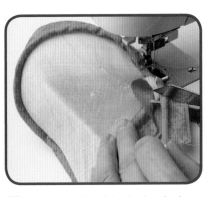

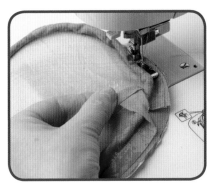

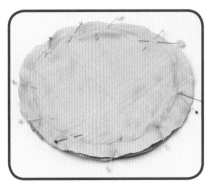

5 As you get back to the beginning, stop with needle down about 4cm (1½in) from the end. Raise the presser foot, unfold the beginning of the piping strip and lay the end inside the fold, trimming the cord so the ends meet.

6 Refold the beginning of the strip to encase the end, then continue stitching through all layers round to the start of the stitching.

7 Lay the cushion front right side up on a flat surface and place the cushion back on top, right side down with the outer edges matching. Pin at right angles.

8 Using a zipper foot, turn the work over and stitch round the edges so the cushion front is uppermost and you can see the previous stitching. If possible, move the needle position to the left so it is as close as possible to the piping. Sew round the edges. Leave a 7cm (2¾in) gap for turning through if you are working with a single back, as here, or ensure the zip is open for a zipped back.

9 Press and trim back the seam allowance, leaving the opening untrimmed.

10 Snip diagonally in towards the seam before turning the cushion right sides out.

11 Stuff the cushion and slip stitch to close the opening. I have added a toning button to the centre of this pincushion.

PERFECTLY PIPED PILLOW

Revamp your décor with a collection of new pillow covers. Piping adds a professional touch and a pretty contrast.

Finished size: 40cm (15¾in) square

1 From patterned fabric cut the pillow front and back pieces as follows: 25cm (10in) square from the main printed cotton; two pieces 40 x 22cm (15¾ x 8½in) for the pillow back; and two 5cm (2in) wide strips cut on the bias (if you are making your own piping). Cut enough to join into one length of 170cm (67in).

2 From the contrast fabrics, cut the borders as follows: from the first fabric, two strips of 25 x 7cm (10 x 2¾in); from the second fabric, two strips of 40 x 7cm (15¾ x 2¾in).

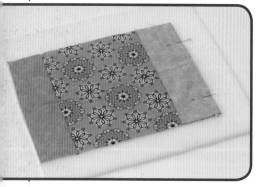

3 Lay the wadding on a flat surface and centre the printed 25cm (10in) square on top, right side up. Pin one short contrast strip to the left edge of the printed square, right sides together and stitch through all layers. Open out the border strip and press. Repeat for the other strip along the right edge.

4 Add the long border strips to the remaining two edges of the printed square, again right sides together and stitching through all layers. Open out the borders and press (inset). Trim the wadding to size if needed.

5 Place the two back pieces right sides together and place the zip centred along one long edge. Mark the top and bottom of the zip opening as shown, then put the zip aside. Pin the back pieces and stitch the seam from the side to the first mark. Reverse stitch to secure, then increase the stitch length to the longest possible to machine baste the zip opening. Baste to within 5cm (2in) of the other mark. Cut the thread. Finish the seam with a regular stitch length from the second mark to the side. Press the seam allowances open and then neaten the edges by zigzag stitching close to the edge.

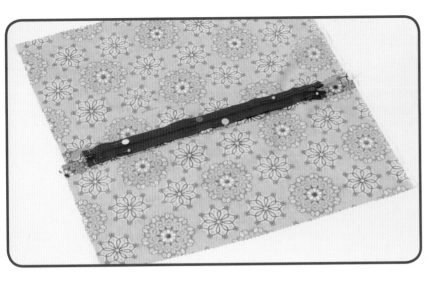

6 Place the back pieces right side down on a flat surface. Position the zip centrally along the basted seam so the teeth are over the seam and the zip pull is at the end that has been left partially unstitched. Pin and baste (tack) in position down both sides of the zip tape. Turn the piece over. Attach the zipper foot.

7 Starting at the bottom end at the seam, and with the back pieces right side up, stitch three or four stitches (see main picture) and then pivot to stitch up the right side, following the basting stitches as a guide. When you get near the zip pull, stop with the needle down and raise the presser foot so you can ease the zip pull behind the foot (see inset). Continue to the top, again pivot and stitch to the centre seam. Repeat for the other side. Unpick the basting stitches in the zip opening and open the zip. Press carefully.

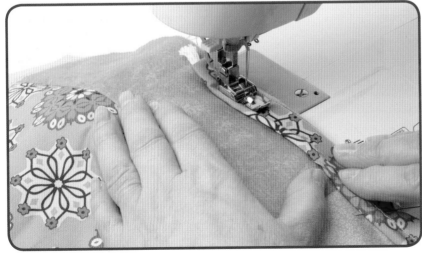

8 Pin the piping to the pillow front, matching the raw edges of the piping fabric to the edge of the right side of the pillow front. Start pinning in the middle of one edge. When you start stitching, begin 4cm (1½in) from the start of the piping and use the zipper foot.

9 At the corners, clip into the piping fabric so the cord will fold smoothly round. Keep the zipper foot butted up to the piping cord and pivot the fabric with the needle down at the corner. Machine stitch the piping in place all the way round.

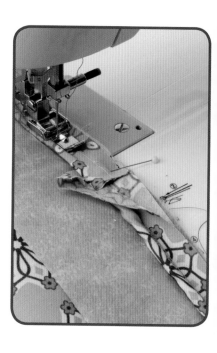

10 Where the two ends meet, either overlap the ends off the edge or join self-made piping as shown in steps 5–6, page 61.

11 Place the pillow back right side up on a flat surface with the zip open and then place the front right side down on top, matching the edges. With the pillow front uppermost, pin and stitch all the way round, stitching as close to the piping cord as possible by moving the needle position to the left. Use the previous stitching which holds the piping in place as a guide and stitch to the left of it. At the corners, stop with the needle down, raise the presser foot and pivot the fabric slightly, then lower the presser foot and take a couple of stitches. Repeat until you can stitch the next side. Continue in this manner around the pillow cover.

12 Trim the seam allowances, cutting the corners at an angle to reduce the bulk in the seams. Press and turn through. Press again and then insert the cushion pad through the zipped opening.

Opposite and left
The finished pillow.

HEMMING WAYS

Two of the easiest and most useful hems are the blind hem and the double top stitched hem. The blind hem is virtually invisible – hence the name, whereas the double top stitched hem has stitching showing on the right side.

Blind hemming

The aim of a blind hem is for the stitching to be invisible on the right side of the garment. In fashions, this hem should also retain a soft rounded edge, so do not press the actual garment edge, just the stitched area. A machine-stitched blind hem is very quick to complete, but does leave a very tiny ladder-like stitch showing on the right side of the fabric. Use a thread colour to closely match the fabric and this will be virtually invisible.

Check your user's manual to see whether one of the feet you have is a blind hem foot. This generally has a bar to the right of the centre of the foot. This bar protrudes below the foot and lines up against the folded edge of the fabric to help guide the fabric straight.

Preparing the fabric

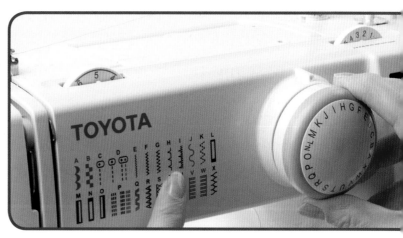

1 Fold the hem allowance up and press lightly. Tuck the raw edge under and press again. (Note that if you are working on thick fabric, neaten the raw edge of fabric and only turn up once). Keeping the hem allowance folded, turn it back underneath to the right side of fabric so that there is at least 12mm (½in) of the hem allowance to the right.

2 Select the blind hem stitch – this will either have a straight stitch to the right with an occasionally zigzag stitch to the left, or a very small zigzag stitch running down, with a larger zigzag to the left. If your machine has both, the straight stitch version is for woven fabrics (although either could be used for these) and the wavy version for knit fabrics.

3 Place the fabric under the foot so that the straight stitch is stitching on the hem allowance close to the fold of the main fabric. The zigzag will then go into the fold every time to anchor the hem in place. Check with a few stitches first that they are catching as they should, then continue with the hem.

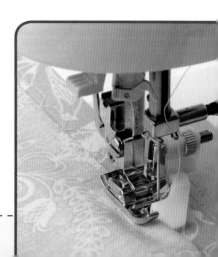

4 The finished stitching is shown left. Once stitched, turn the hem allowance to the wrong side and press along the stitched seam (leaving the actual edge of the project unpressed so it has a slightly rounded edge). On the right side there is a tiny ladder stitch, but it should be virtually invisible if a good thread match has been used (inset).

Stitching in the ditch

As well as using the foot for blind hemming, you can use it for 'stitching in the ditch' which is when you sew in the seam on the right side of two joined pieces, for instance at waistbands or when attaching binding. You can also use it to add trims.

Double top stitched hem

This is a very quick hemming method and one used on clothing, pocket tops and soft furnishings such as curtains and tablecloths. As mentioned on page 35, top stitching is simply stitching that shows on the right side. A double hem is one that has the hem allowance folded twice to encase the raw edge, so it is double thickness. Working from the right side, stitch close to the inner fold through all thicknesses.

   If you prefer not to have the stitching visible, simply use the blind hem technique above, or hand stitch the hem.

CAFÉ CURTAIN

This style of window dressing is perfect for kitchens and dining rooms – allowing light in while providing privacy. Our curtain has pleats and tab tops.

Finished size: This depends on the window to be dressed. Allow twice the width and half the window height.

Calculating how much fabric is required

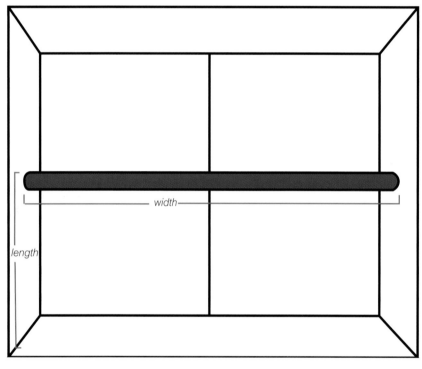

Diagram 1

Width x 2 + seam allowances + hems
Length + hem allowances

1 First decide at what height you wish to hang the curtains. If you have a plain window, about halfway down is perfect and this is the height to put the pole. If you have windows with a horizontal bar across them, use this as the position for the pole. **For the length,** measure from the pole position to the windowsill. Add 16cm (6¼in) for the hems top and bottom. **For the width,** measure the length of the pole and double it. Add approximately 8–10cm (3⅛–4in) for seams and side hems (2cm/¾in per side seam and 4cm/1½in for French seams if joining pieces). It is likely that you will need to join fabric widths to get the total width required. To determine how much fabric this requires, divide the total width needed by the width of your chosen fabric. This will give you the amount of 'drops' or panels needed. Each drop will be the length calculated as above. To buy fabric, multiply the number of drops required by the length.

Example:
Window length from pole to sill: 60cm (23¾in) + 16cm (6¼in) for hems = 76cm (30in).

Window width 107cm (42in) x 2 = 214cm (84⅜in) + 8cm (3⅛in) for seams = 222cm (87½in).

To get the full 222cm (87½in) width required, we needed at least 2 drops (lengths). Our fabric was 112cm (44in) wide x 2 drops = 224cm (88in), so we needed two drops of 76cm (30in). Total fabric needed for curtain = 1.52m (60in).

Note: More fabric would have been needed if it had a noticeable pattern and therefore 'pattern repeat'. To determine the extra required, measure the pattern repeat and add this to the length of each drop required.

As the extra width we got was just 2cm (¾in) more than required to get our total of 222cm (87½in), we just took slightly bigger pleats at either side.

Sewing the widths together with a French seam

2 Cut the number of drops required to the right length. Trim away the selvedges on each piece (often the sevedges are more tightly woven and can distort the side seams).

Tip

If it is difficult to see which is the right side of the fabric, decide which you prefer then chalk mark the reverse on all pieces to ensure you use the same side every time.

Diagram 2

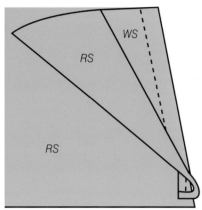

3 Sew the widths together to create one wide curtain piece, using a French seam (see Diagram 2 above). First sew the seam, taking a 1cm (³⁄₈in) seam allowance, with wrong sides together. Trim the seam allowance to 6mm (¼in) as shown.

4 Turn over so the right sides are together and the seam is on the edge. Press and sew again, 1cm (³⁄₈in) from the edge, neatly encasing the raw edges so the back of the curtain looks as neat as the front.

Making the top edge

5 For the top edge, cut strips of interfacing 5cm (2in) deep to make up a length equal to the the total curtain width. Iron it on to the wrong side of the curtain, 1cm (³⁄₈in) from the top edge. Once cooled, turn under the 1cm (³⁄₈in) top edge and press then fold the top down (see inset) a further 5cm (2in) and press. Stitch close to the top edge and again close to the lower fold (see main picture).

Hemming

6 Neaten the side edges of the curtain by taking a double hem. Fold under 1cm (³⁄₈in), then again another 1cm (³⁄₈in), encasing the raw edge. Top stitch in place. Press.

7 To make a blind hem, fold up the hem by 5cm (2in), then fold again by the same amount. Fold the hem allowance back on itself as shown in step 1, page 66, so that 13mm (½in) of the allowance protrudes to the right. Select the blind hem foot and blind hem stitch and then sew with the straight stitch on the hem allowance and the zigzag stitch catching the curtain to the left.

Making pleats

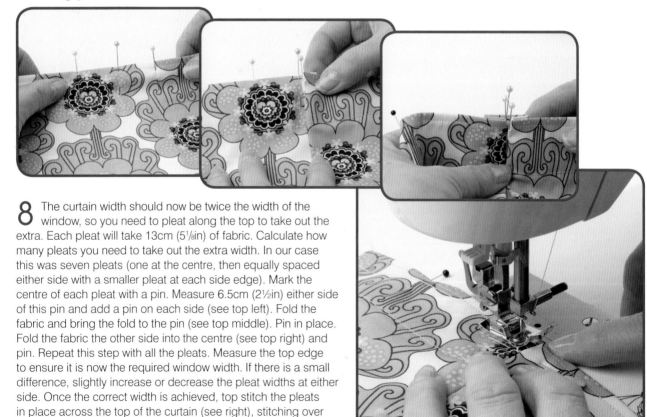

8 The curtain width should now be twice the width of the window, so you need to pleat along the top to take out the extra. Each pleat will take 13cm (5⅛in) of fabric. Calculate how many pleats you need to take out the extra width. In our case this was seven pleats (one at the centre, then equally spaced either side with a smaller pleat at each side edge). Mark the centre of each pleat with a pin. Measure 6.5cm (2½in) either side of this pin and add a pin on each side (see top left). Fold the fabric and bring the fold to the pin (see top middle). Pin in place. Fold the fabric the other side into the centre (see top right) and pin. Repeat this step with all the pleats. Measure the top edge to ensure it is now the required window width. If there is a small difference, slightly increase or decrease the pleat widths at either side. Once the correct width is achieved, top stitch the pleats in place across the top of the curtain (see right), stitching over the previous stitching. Stitch again 5cm (2in) down, over the previous stitching.

Making tabs

9 Using the contrast fabric, cut the same number of tabs as pleats, each 9cm (3½in) wide x 24cm (9½in) long. Fuse interfacing to the wrong side of each piece. Fold each tab in half, right sides together and stitch along the long edge. Trim the seam allowance and turn through. Refold so the seam is in the centre as shown and press. Tuck the raw ends inside and press.

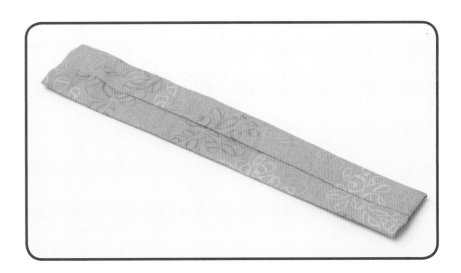

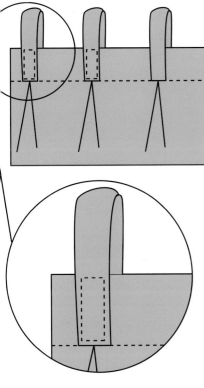

Diagram 3

10 Fold the tabs in half with the seam on the inside, and then pin them to the front and back of the curtain top over the pleats. Increase the stitch length to 3 and using a jeans needle, stitch through all layers in a box shape to secure the tabs in place, neatly stitching the open ends of the tabs closed at the same time (see Diagram 3, left).

Adding self–covered buttons

Self-coverable buttons come in packs with instructions for use on the reverse. They are very simple to use and mean you can have buttons that coordinate perfectly with your project.

- Cut a circle of fabric to the size shown on the reverse of the packaging (about twice the diameter of the button). If it is a lightweight or see-through fabric, add interfacing first.

- Stitch round the outside edge with a long hand stitch and pull up to gather, placing the button top in the centre of the wrong side. Pull up the thread until the circle fits tightly around the button. Tie off the ends.

- Clip on the button back, covering the raw edges of the fabric circle.

11 Hand stitch the buttons in place on the front of the tabs. You are now ready to loop the tabs over the pole and put up the curtain.

Opposite
The finished Café Curtains.

QUILTING

The term quilting describes the stitching that holds two or more layers together, usually sandwiching a layer of wadding (or batting) to create a thick quilt or coverlet that is decorative and warm.

A quilt will usually have three layers – a top, the layer of wadding (batting) and a backing fabric. To make sure the layers all stay together, they are quilted. This might be straight lines stitched 'in the ditch' (stitched along previous seams so that the stitching is virtually invisible) or stitched with patterns, grids, swirls, stippling or vermicelli patterns (meandering free-motion stitching; see page 84).

Walking foot

When quilting thick layers, it is advisable and helpful to use a walking foot (also known as an even-feed foot). This is designed to feed the layers evenly. A walking foot has its own feed dogs and an arm on the right which goes over the needle bar. As the needle goes up and down, so do the feed dogs on the walking foot, helping to 'walk over' the fabric as they work in conjunction with the feed dogs on the machine.

This foot is also useful for sewing stretchy fabric, or when it is essential to match stripes and checks, as it ensures the layers are fed through evenly. It can also be used to sew sticky fabrics like vinyl or plastic.

Quilting step by step

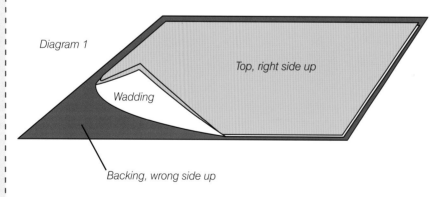

Diagram 1

Top, right side up

Wadding

Backing, wrong side up

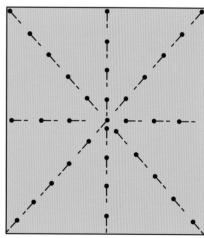

Diagram 2

1 Prepare the quilt layers: the backing fabric wrong side up, then the layer of wadding, then the quilt top, right side up (see Diagram 1). Pin or baste (tack) the layers together, starting in the centre and working out to the sides, smoothing the layers as you go (see Diagram 2).

2 If preferred, mark the quilt lines with chalk or water soluble or fade-away pen. Alternatively, set up the machine for free-motion sewing (see page 82).

3 If quilting in straight lines or patterns, fit the walking foot, ensuring that the arm on the right fits over the needle bar. Increase the stitch length to 3–3.5mm (9) to accommodate the thick layers of fabric. Start quilting along the centre marked line. Continue stitching along each marked line, working from the centre outwards, stitching each line in the same direction.

The walking foot with the arm over the needle bar.

Quilting guide

Many sewing machines come with this nifty gadget, which is basically a metal bar with a right angle and a curved end (see Diagram 3). The straight part of the bar slots into the back of a presser foot holder, or into a groove on the back of a walking foot. After the first row of stitching is made, the bar can be moved to the left or right to determine the spacing between rows of stitching, with the curved end sitting over the first line of quilting to ensure the next row is perfectly parallel. As you move across the quilt, the quilting guide rests on the previous row of stitching so that all lines will be equally spaced.

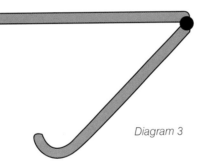

Diagram 3

The quilting guide in the back of the foot holder.

Finishing the quilt

Quilts are usually finished with quilt binding or bias binding around the edges. This neatly encases the raw edges. Quilt binding is a strip of fabric, folded in half lengthways with wrong sides together. Bias binding has both long edges turned to the centre on the wrong side before being folded in half.

Bindings can be bought ready-made in a variety of colours, or you can make your own from any suitable fabric to ensure it perfectly suits your project. Generally you need to cut a fabric strip twice the finished width required. Thus for a 2.5cm (1in) wide binding, you need strips of 5cm (2in).

See pages 78–80 for instructions on attaching quilt or bias binding.

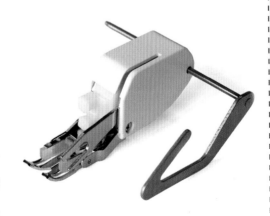

The quilting guide in the walking foot.

QUILTED POT HOLDER

Make these nifty pot holders to match your kitchen décor and prevent burnt fingers.

Finished size: 23 x 16cm (9 x 6¼in)

1 From the cotton, compressed fleece wadding and interfacing cut:
Two main pieces 24 x 18cm (9½ x 7in)
Two pocket pieces 13 x 18cm (5⅛ x 7in).

2 Trim the interfacing by 1cm (³/₈in) all the way round, centre on the wrong side of the cotton pieces and fuse in place with a hot iron (use a press cloth to protect the fabric).

You will need

Fat quarter or 36 x 48cm (14 x 19in) of printed cotton

36 x 48cm (14 x 19in) of medium-weight iron-on interfacing

36 x 48cm (14 x 19in) of compressed fleece wadding

Pack of bias binding

Thread to match fabric

Walking foot and quilting guide (if available)

Water soluble pen

Cutting out

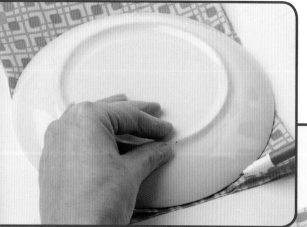

3 Lay one piece of compressed fleece wadding on a flat surface and a main fabric piece on top, matching the edges. Using a plate and a water soluble pen, draw a curve round the corners at one end to give a nice rounded edge. Repeat for the other compressed fleece wadding and main fabric and then the pocket sections, and cut them all out so all have the curved edge at one end.

Quilting a grid

Walking foot and quilting guide

Using a walking foot will help feed layers evenly and together. If you have one, add the quilting guide into the back of the walking foot and stitch perfectly parallel rows with the guide on the previous row each time. If no guide is available, chalk mark lines in a grid and follow those as you stitch.

TIP

Watch the quilting guide as you stitch each row, not the needle – it helps keep the lines evenly spaced.

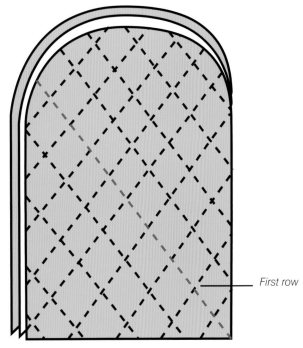

First row

Diagram 1

4 Layer the main pieces as follows: the main fabric wrong side up, the two pieces of wadding, then the main fabric wrong side down so that the curved ends are together and the side edges match. Pin through all layers. Machine quilt in place, starting diagonally across the centre as shown in Diagram 1. Start the next row to the left about 2.5cm (1in) from the first row. Continue stitching in rows to the left of the centre. Turn the piece up the other way and stitch to the right of the central diagonal line. Then turn the work at right angles to stitch in the opposite direction to make a cross-grid. Once the piece is quilted, trim the outside edges evenly.

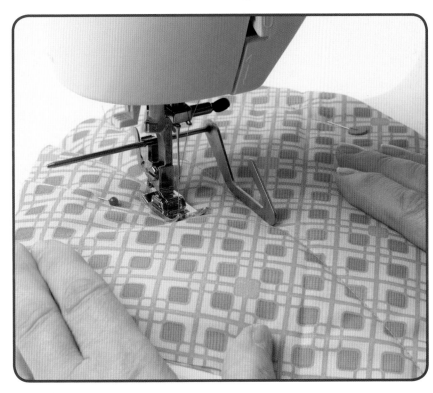

5 Layer and quilt the pocket pieces as in step 4 above. Trim the edges evenly.

Adding bias binding

6 Fold bias binding around the straight edge of the pocket piece and pin it in in place. Select a decorative stitch and stitch through all layers, encasing the raw edges of the pocket as you go.

7 Pin the pocket to the curved end of the main piece, matching the edges. Machine stitch in place.

Making a hanging loop

8 Cut a 9cm (3½in) length of bias binding, fold it in half lengthways and stitch along the centre with a decorative stitch in a contrasting thread. Fold it in half to form a loop and pin it to the centre of the straight edge of the pot holder, with the raw edges matching as shown. Stitch across the ends about 5mm (¼in) from the raw edges.

Finishing the edges

9 Open out the bias binding and pin then stitch it to the underside of the pot holder, starting in the middle of one straight edge. Leave the first 2cm (¾in) or so of the binding unstitched for turning later. When you get to the bottom corner, stitch to within 5mm (¼in) of the end, reverse stitch to secure and take the work out of the machine. Fold the binding at right angles to the stitched seam (see left), then fold it back down along the next edge to mitre the corner (see below). Place the work under the needle and stitch from close to the fold in the binding. Continue to the next corner, catching the loop in place as you go and repeat the mitre for this corner.

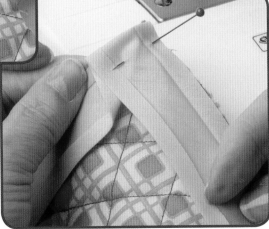

10 Continue until the ends come together and then lap ends as shown, first turning up the raw edge of the underlap. Lay the overlap on top and lap by 1cm (³/8in). Trim off the excess binding and complete the stitching.

11 Trim the seam allowances evenly and turn the bias binding over the right side. Select the same decorative stitch as used on the pocket and, working from the right side, stitch the binding in place.

12 At the corners, fold the excess binding into a neat diagonal line and pin in place. (Note that you can also hand slip stitch the corners of the binding together if preferred). Stitch up to the corner, pivot and continue.

A pair of Quilted Pot Holders.

FREE MOTION

Most sewing machines will allow you to sew free-hand or free motion. This means the feed dogs (little teeth that protrude through the throat plate) are put out of action. Normally they move backwards and forwards to help feed the fabric through the machine as you stitch. When lowered (or covered) they do not effect the movement of the fabric, which means you can move it around by hand in any direction. Hence the terms free motion or freehand.

The stitches are formed as usual, with the top and bobbin threads, but how long or short the stitches are depends on how fast and far you move the fabric. Move it quickly and you get bigger stitches, move it slowly and stitches will be smaller.

Free motion is often used by quilters to quilt their projects. There are some traditional free-motion stitches such as vermicelli (a meandering stitch) and stippling (covering an area with randomly directed stitching), or you can create your own pattern. By working freehand, you control the direction so you can work all over a piece, rather than stitching in lines.

Darning/embroidery foot

As well as lowering the feed dogs, you will need a darning/embroidery foot. This foot does not sit firmly on the fabric as other feet do; it gently rests on it as you stitch, raising again as the needle comes up. It often has a spring to help the movement and may have an open toe at the front or a oval aperture. There are many styles of darning/embroidery foot but to start with, buy a basic one suitable for the make and model of your sewing machine.

Tip

On some machines it is possible to stitch without a foot at all. Lower the presser foot lever to engage the tension discs and sew, taking very great care not to get your fingers too close to the needle!

Fabric support

It is advisable to add stabiliser to the fabric when free-motion stitching to provide stability and to help you move the fabric freely. There are different types of stabiliser available ranging from the most widely used tear-away stabiliser (once stitched, you tear away the excess), to ultra-fine or heavy-duty soluble stabilisers, or heat-away or sticky-backed stabilisers.

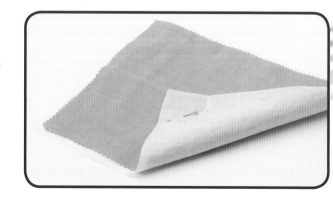

Hooping

Working in a hoop makes it easier to move the work in any direction and helps keep fingers away from the needle. It also helps keep the fabric taut, which is essential if you don't want the fabric to pucker when stitched.

To hoop the fabric, cut the fabric and stabiliser slightly larger than the outer hoop. Lay the stabiliser and fabric, right side up, on top of the larger hoop and then push the smaller hoop in position. Tighten the screw to keep the fabric taut.

Getting started

1 Attach the darning/embroidery foot and lower the feed dogs. Usually there is a little diagram with a lever and teeth either on the back of the machine below the needle area, or under the needle at the front. Check your user's manual. Some very basic models may have a little cover to place over the feed dogs instead.

2 Reduce the stitch length to 0. You control the stitch length by how quickly or slowly you move the fabric.

3 Start by stitching a couple of stitches on the spot to anchor the thread, then, pressing the foot control for fast stitching, start moving the fabric in slow, even movements. Try straight lines, wavy lines and circles. Once you have mastered this, you can create flowers and other designs.

Tip
Always sew a few stitches on top of each other to finish off before moving on to a different part of fabric or completing your design.

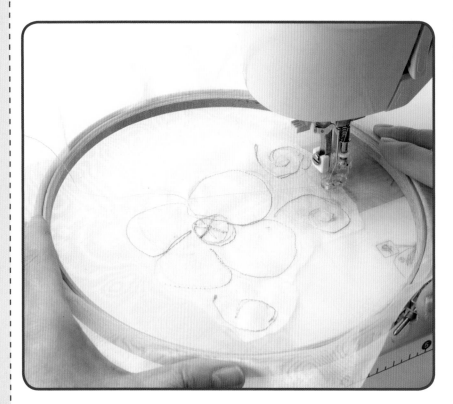

Draw shapes such as swirls and flowers on the fabric or the stabiliser backing and follow them with your stitching.

Quilt a project with a free-hand meandering stitch such as vermicelli or stippling. It is quick to do and there is no right or wrong design. Vermicelli is supposed to be a series of meandering, wavy swirls which do not cross or touch each other.

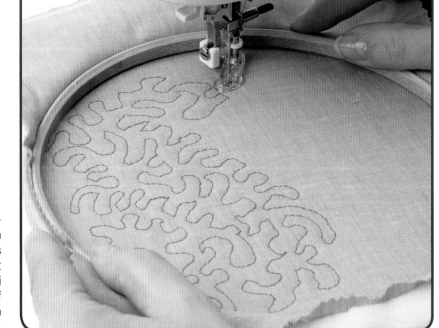

Tip

To make sewing easier, you don't have to finish the ends and cut the thread whenever you want to move to a different part of the fabric. Simply sew a few stitches on the spot, then raise the foot, pull the hoop to move it to another area of the fabric, lower the foot and carry on sewing. Once you have finished, just cut the threads that you don't need.

Detail of the free-motion stitching on organza in the Swirls and Flowers Scarf project (see page 86).

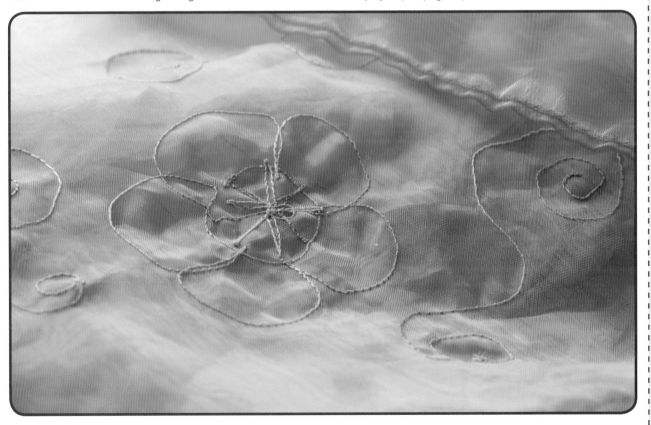

SWIRLS AND FLOWERS SCARF

Turn a simple length of delicate chiffon into a couture scarf with a little free-motion stitching and narrow seams.

Finished size: 140 x 20cm wide (55 x 8in)

Shaping the ends

Diagram 1

Fold

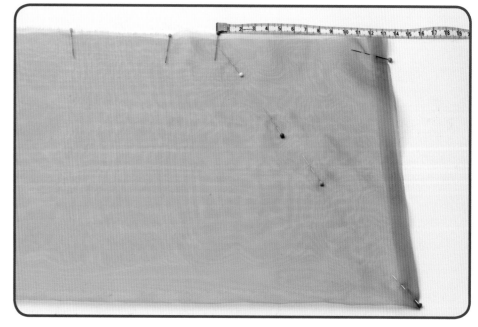

1 Fold the fabric lengthways with right sides together and pin carefully; flimsy fabric like this chiffon tends to shift easily, making it difficult to sew neatly, so plenty of pins are required. Along the pinned side seam (see the top of Diagram 1 above), mark 13cm (5in) from the ends and draw a diagonal line from the mark to the opposite corner to angle the scarf ends.

Tip

Add a small 3cm (1¼in) strip of soluble stabiliser under the start of the seam to prevent the fine fabric being pulled into the feed dogs. Once the seam is stitched, this can be washed away.

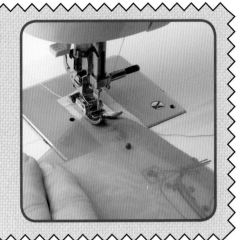

2 Sew the ends and the side seam, taking a 15mm (⅝in) seam allowance and leaving a turning gap in the centre of the long edge of approximately 15cm (6in).

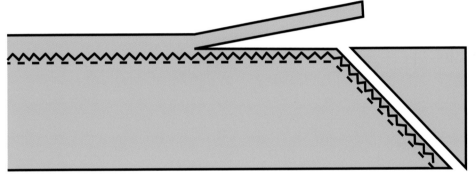

Diagram 2

3 Change to a small zigzag stitch. If possible, reduce the stitch width to 2mm (¹⁄₁₆in) and sew again close to the first stitching. Trim the seam allowance close to the stitching (see Diagram 2 above and photograph). Press the seam to embed the stitching and turn through, pushing the end points out with a point turner or knitting needle. Press again.

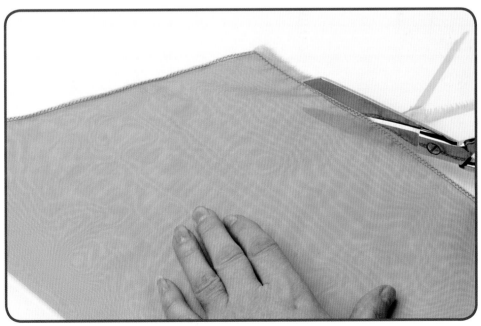

4 Draw swirls and flower shapes on soluble stabiliser using a chalk pencil or water soluble pen. Cut them into groups and place them randomly across the scarf. Make sure the pieces of soluble stabiliser are slightly bigger than the area to be stitched (see Diagram 3).

Diagram 3

5 Set your machine up for free-motion stitching: drop or cover the feed dogs (check your user's manual) and attach the darning/embroidery foot. Turn the stitch length to 0, as you will control the length of the stitch you make by how fast or slowly you move the fabric.

Tip
Working in an embroidery hoop makes it much easier to follow outlines.

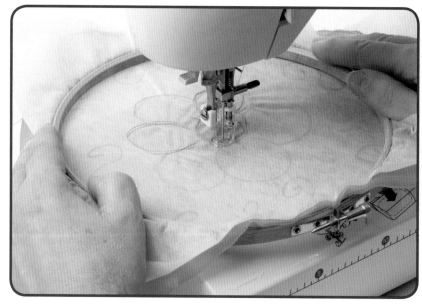

6 Fit the scarf in an embroidery hoop with the soluble stabiliser on top. Thread the bobbin and top with machine embroidery thread and start free motion stitching, moving the fabric slowly, following your drawn outlines.

7 Once the scarf is covered with free-motion stitching, wash away the soluble stabiliser and allow the scarf to dry. Press carefully with the iron on a silk setting and with a press cloth over the scarf to protect it.

Opposite
The finished Swirls and Flowers Scarf. This one is in a slightly different shade of green for a subtle, elegant look.

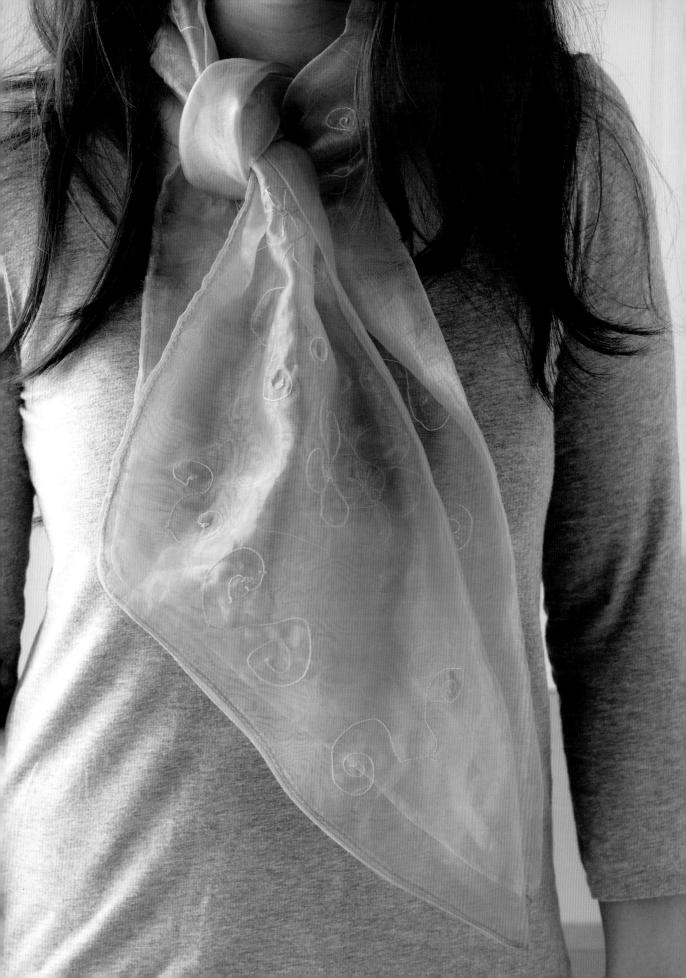

TWIN NEEDLES

Using a twin needle can create some fabulous decorative finishes with pretty top stitching and even pin tucks.

A twin needle has two needles attached to one shank, so they are inserted into the needle holder in exactly the same way as a single needle. There are different sizes of needle such as size 75 (11) for lightweight fabrics and size 90 (14) for more heavyweight fabrics and there are also sharps or ballpoint needles for different types of fabric. You can also choose the distance between the needles ranging from 1.6mm ($^1/_{16}$in) to 4mm ($^1/_8$in). Which you use will depend on the fabric being stitched and the technique required. A good general-purpose twin needle is a 1.6mm ($^1/_{16}$in) size 75 (11).

How a twin needle stitches

You will need two top threads, one for each needle. Most machines can do twin needle stitching and will come with two thread spindles. If you only have one, you can wind two bobbins and place them on top of each other on the one thread spindle.

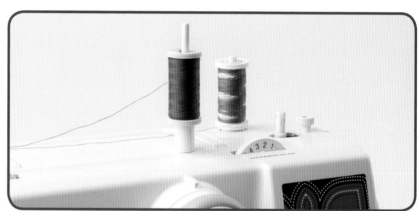

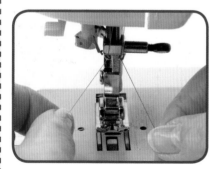

1 Thread both reels through the threading path together until you get to the final hook above the needle. Some machines will have a hook to the left and right so you can place one thread through each, as shown. Alternatively, thread one through the final hook and leave the other loose.

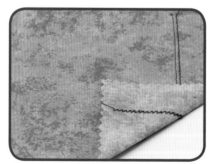

2 Choose a straight stitch, stretch stitch or small zigzag stitch to start with. The top threads form two perfectly parallel rows of stitching while underneath the bobbin thread creates a zigzag as it goes from one needle to the other.

Tip
On lightweight fabrics, the fabric might gather slightly between the needles, causing a little ridge. To counter this you can add interfacing to the underside and loosen the tension (decrease to 2–3). Always try samples on a scrap of fabric first.

Top stitching

Use a twin needle to recreate a 'cover stitch' hem, which is the type of hem you often see on shop-bought garments. This has two parallel rows of top stitching as in the sample shown right.

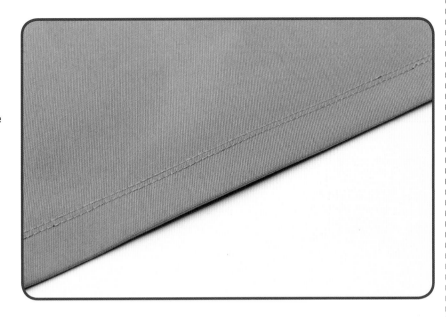

Decorative work

Experiment with the stitching. Remember that you have two needles to go through the presser foot aperture and throat plate so do not choose stitches that require wide swings of the needle. Try out the whole sequence of the stitch by turning the balance wheel by hand to ensure that the needles don't hit the foot during the stitching. Once happy, use the foot pedal as usual.

Try using different colour threads in the top too; it can add another dimension to the results.

Samples of decorative stitching using a twin needle.

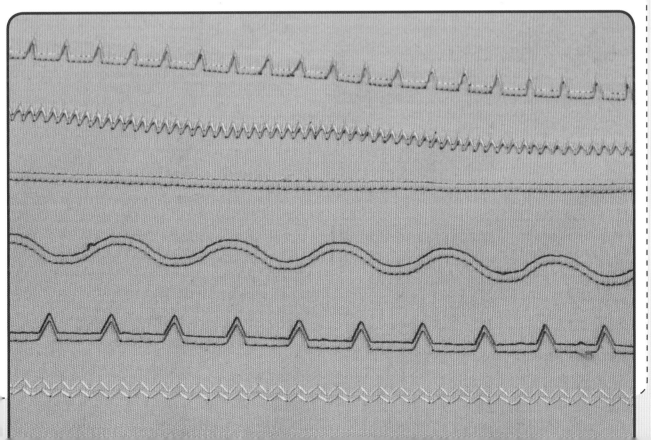

Pin tucks

Pin tucks are very narrow tucks formed by taking small folds of fabric. A quick way of making perfect pin tucks is to use a twin needle and pin tuck foot, although you can do them without the special foot, just using the regular zigzag foot. They can also be corded (with a length of cord laid inside the fold) to make them more prominent.

Pin tuck foot

These come with three, five or seven grooves on the underside, into which the fabric runs. They are often packaged in pairs, one with smaller grooves for lightweight fabrics and the other with larger grooves for heavier fabrics.

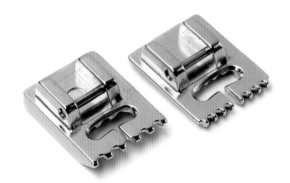

Choosing needles and tension

First choose your needle. On lightweight fabrics use a fine size 60 (9) twin needle with a narrow gap between the needles, such as 1.6mm (¹/₁₆in). For heavyweight fabrics, use a size 90 (14) needle with 4mm (³/₁₆in) gap. If sewing jersey, use a ballpoint or stretch needle. Increase the tension to 7–8 so that the zigzag bobbin thread pulls up and causes the ridge between the twin needles.

1 Mark the position of the first tuck by drawing a chalk line along the entire length.

2 Attach the pin tuck foot and change the needle to the appropriate twin needle. Select the centre needle position. Increase the tension to approximately 7 on the tension dial.

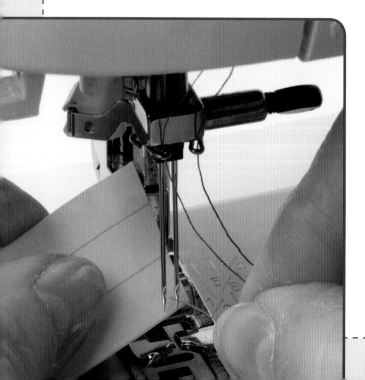

3 Thread the two top threads through the thread path and use a matching thread in the bobbin.

Tips

To avoid the top threads tangling, place one clockwise on the spindle and the other anticlockwise.

To help you see more clearly when threading the twin needles, hold a piece of paper behind the needles as shown left.

4 Position the fabric under the presser foot, with the marked line in the centre of the foot so the needles will stitch either side. Stitch the tuck to the end.

5 Move the fabric so the first tuck sits in a groove to the right or left of centre and stitch the next tuck in the same direction.

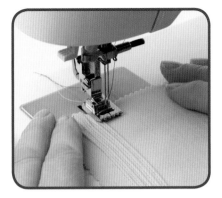

Tip

Try out tuck composition on a fabric remnant to see whether you want them very close together, or evenly spaced a groove width apart, or use the edge of the presser foot as a guide.

Sewing pin tucks without a pin tuck foot

Mark the first tuck position as above. Then, for subsequent tucks, use the presser foot as a guide, running the previous tuck down the inner or outer edge of the presser foot, depending on how closely together you want the tucks to form.

Corded pin tucks

Sometimes you may want the pin tucks to really stand out. To create more definite tucks, you can feed a fine cord under the presser foot to sit between the needles so that when the tuck is formed, it is held in place by the zigzag of the bobbin thread.

Raised pin tucks made using cords.

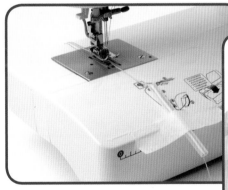

A straw taped to the machine ready to keep the cord in place while sewing.

To help guide the cord in place, thread it through a length of straw taped in place in front of the machine. Then guide it with your hands, either side of the cord as you sew.

Tip

Some pin tuck feet come with a little cord guide to clip on to the front of the throat plate. Check with your sewing machine dealer to see which works with your machine.

RETRO APRON

Make this pretty apron with a vintage flavour by adding pin tucks and shaping to the bib and ruffles to the hemline.

Finished size: bib 25cm (10in) wide, apron length 71cm (28in)

Cutting out

1 From the main fabric cut an over-sized bib piece 40 x 30cm (16 x 12in). This will be pin tucked and then cut to size. Also cut the skirt of the apron 46cm (18in) square.

2 From the other fabric cut:
Two waistband panels 46cm (18in) long x 7cm (2¾in) wide.
Three ties 71cm (28in) long x 7cm (2¾in) wide.
Two pocket pieces 16cm (6¼in) square.
One hem ruffle strip, 240 x 11cm (94½in x 4¼in).
One bib ruffle strip 75cm x 7cm (29½ x 2¾in).

Pin tucking the bib

3 Fold the bib fabric in half lengthways and press to mark the centre. Unfold.

4 Insert the twin needle and thread both reels through the threading path together. Tighten the tension to 7. Starting at the marked fold line, stitch the first pin tuck just right of the fold line. Stitch another just left of the fold line. To create the next pin tuck, go back to the top of the bib with the first pin tuck in the left groove of the pin tuck foot and stitch the next tuck. Next start from the bottom of the bib and stitch another pin tuck the other side of the central two. Continue in this manner, working either side of the centre until you have stitched five either side of the two central tucks.

Tip

If you do not have a twin needle option or pin tuck foot, you can still stitch small tucks. Fold the fabric width-wise as before to mark the centre and press. Keep folded and position under the presser foot so that the right-hand edge of the foot is butted up against the fold of fabric. Make sure the needle is in the raised position and, using the stitch width button, move the needle as far to the right as possible. Stitch the tuck. Continue to fold and stitch tucks either side of central tuck until you have seven tucks.

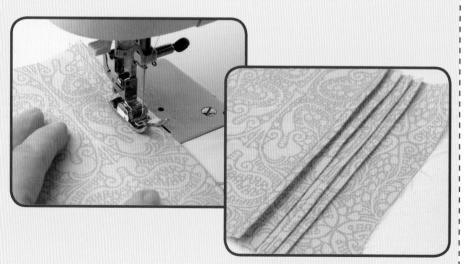

You will need

Two 50cm (19¾in) pieces of 114cm (45in) wide coordinating fabrics

Tea plate

Chalk pencil or water soluble pen

Lightweight iron-on interfacing

Twin needle with 1.6–2mm gap between needles

Pin tuck foot (optional)

Thread to match

Shoelace

Shaping the bib top

5 Cut the bib down to 29cm wide x 30cm (11½ x 12in) high with the pin tucking in the centre. Fold it in half, right sides together and lay it on a flat surface. Position the tea plate as shown and draw round it with chalk pencil or water soluble pen to make a curve either side of the centre, to create the sweetheart shape. Cut out the shape.

Making the ruffle and attaching to the bib

6 Fold the bib ruffle strip in half lengthways, wrong sides together and press. Gather the long raw edges by stitching with the longest machine stitch, or by hand stitching. Pull up the bobbin thread to gather the edge so that it is 29cm (11½in) long to match the top of the bib.

7 Pin the ruffle to the top edge of the bib, right sides together and raw edges matching. Machine stitch in place, taking a 15mm (⅝in) seam allowance. Trim the seam and snip into the V at the centre, close to but not through the stitching.

8 Turn the ruffle up and press it with the seam allowance towards the bib. Set the machine to a small zigzag stitch, and working from the right side, stitch around the top of the bib, catching the seam allowances in place as you go.

9 Turn the side edges of the bib to the wrong side by 1cm (³⁄₈in), then again by 1cm (³⁄₈in). Top stitch in place.

Making the apron skirt

10 Fold the apron skirt section in half, right sides together and using a tea plate again, shape the outer lower edges to curve the bottom hem.

11 Make two pleats in the top of the apron. Measure in 11cm (4¼in) from the left-hand side edge and mark with a pin. Then take a fold in the fabric 2.5cm (1in) from the pin and bring the fold to the pin. Repeat on the other side of the pin. Do the same for the right-hand side of apron. Stitch in place.

Adding the ruffle to the skirt

12 Stitch the short ends of the ruffle pieces together to form one long length and fold this in half, wrong sides together. Press. Use pins to mark the long edge into three equal lengths, then, using the longest stitch possible, sew the long edges together in three sections (see Diagram 1). Pull up the bobbin thread to gather each section until the entire ruffle is the length of the sides and bottom edge of the apron.

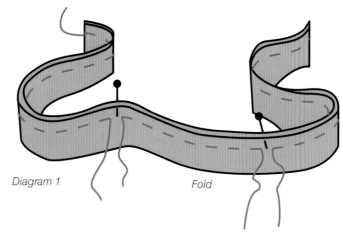

Diagram 1   *Fold*

13 Pin the ruffle to the apron skirt, right sides and raw edges together and stitch it, taking a 15mm (⁵⁄₈in) seam allowance. Turn the ruffle up and press with the seam allowance towards the apron. From the right side, top stitch close to the apron edge with a zigzag stitch as you did for the bib.

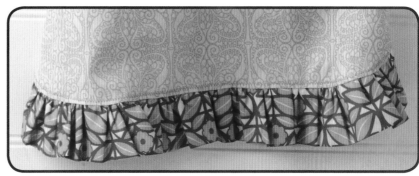

Adding the pocket

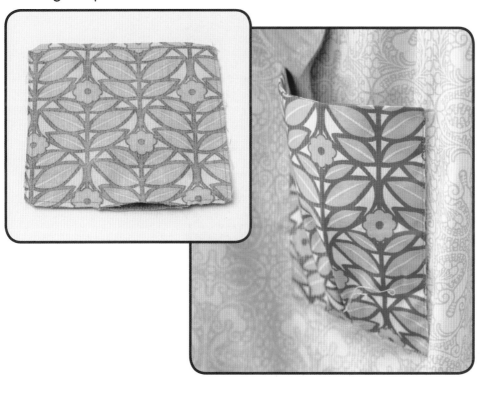

14 Stitch the two pocket pieces right sides together, leaving a turning gap in the lower edge. Clip corners at an angle and turn through. Make a small tuck in the centre bottom edge of the pocket and then pin the pocket to the apron in the desired position. Edge stitch round the sides and bottom, which will stitch up the turning gap as you go. To edge stitch, move the needle as far right as possible and use the edge of the foot as a guide.

Waistbanding

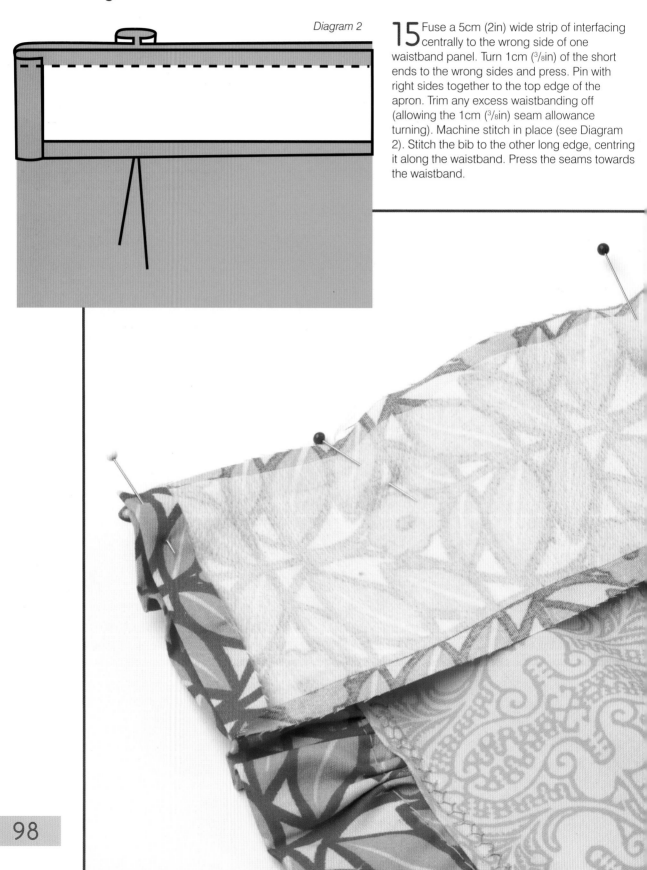

Diagram 2

15 Fuse a 5cm (2in) wide strip of interfacing centrally to the wrong side of one waistband panel. Turn 1cm ($^3/_8$in) of the short ends to the wrong sides and press. Pin with right sides together to the top edge of the apron. Trim any excess waistbanding off (allowing the 1cm ($^3/_8$in) seam allowance turning). Machine stitch in place (see Diagram 2). Stitch the bib to the other long edge, centring it along the waistband. Press the seams towards the waistband.

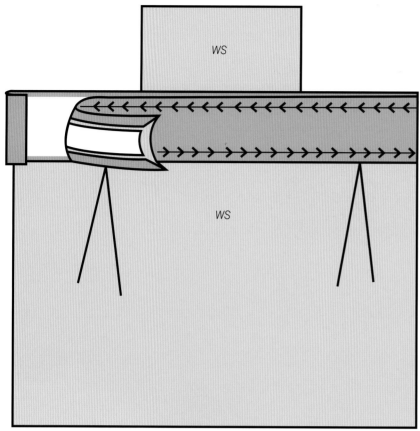

WS

WS

Diagram 3

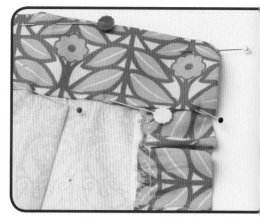

16 Fold the edges of the other waistband panel to the wrong side by 1cm (³⁄₈in) all round and press (again you may need to trim one end of the panel to the correct length). On the wrong side of the apron, pin this panel over the attached waistband, encasing the raw edges and matching the seamlines. Either slip stitch in place at the top and bottom, or use a decorative stitch and machine stitch in place working from the right side (see Diagram 3).

Making the ties

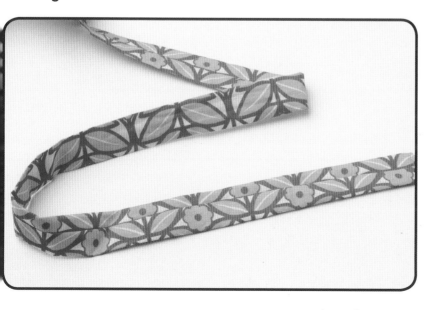

17 Fold the tie fabric strip in half, right sides together. Insert the shoelace into the fold, with a little bit poking out of the top. Stitch across the shoelace and then down the side of the strip. To turn through, pull on the lace, then unpick the stitching that held the lace and use it for the next tie. Refold the tie so the seam is the in the centre and press. Tuck the raw edges inside at one end and top stitch in place. Repeat for the other tie.

18 Slip the raw ends of the ties into the waistband panel. Machine stitch in place down the sides.

19 Make the neck tie as in step 17. Pin it to the wrong side of the bib at the top side edges, adjust the length to suit and then trim off the excess, leaving enough to tuck the raw ends inside the tube. Press and stitch in place.

Opposite and below

The finished Retro Apron.

BOBBIN WORK

Bobbin work is when the main decorative element of the stitching is created by thread wound on to the bobbin. This is done because the thread is too thick or may have a bobbly texture that will not go through the top tension or needle. Using thicker threads in the bobbin, combined with a simple straight or zigzag stitch, creates some pretty patterns that are only revealed when you turn the work over.

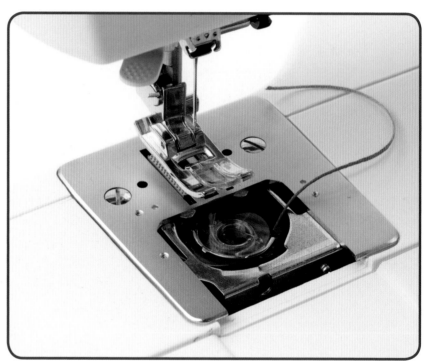

1 Hand wind the thicker thread on to the bobbin, keeping an even tension on the thread as you wind it.

2 Drop the bobbin into the bobbin case without pulling the thread through the tension. It is very important that you do not pull the thicker thread through the bobbin tension – simply drop the bobbin in and leave the thread tail as it lays. Turn the balance wheel by hand to bring up the thread.

3 Place the work face down, so the right side is against the throat plate. Select a simple straight or zigzag stitch and stitch slowly.

Samples of bobbin work with the plainer stitching on one side and the decorative part with the bobbin thread showing on the other.

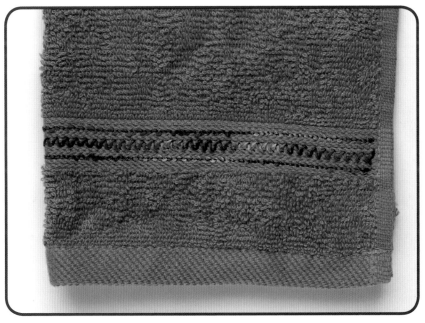

Bobbin work on a face cloth.

DECORATED GUEST TOWEL

Make guests feel welcome with a towel that you've personalised with appliqué and bobbin work. You can decorate a face cloth to match.

You will need

Towel

Crochet yarn or embroidery thread (we used a variegated thread)

Remnants of fabric for the appliqué

Double-sided fusible web

Machine embroidery thread to match appliqué fabric and another to contrast

Tear-away stabiliser

Appliqué

Diagram 1   Fusible web

WS

1 Press 10cm (4in) square pieces of fusible web on to the reverse of the fabric remnants. Draw the flower heads on the paper backing and cut the flowers out. See Diagram 1 left.

2 Peel off the paper backing and place the flowers on the towel. Iron in place. Pin some tear-away stabiliser behind the flower positions, on the other side of the towel.

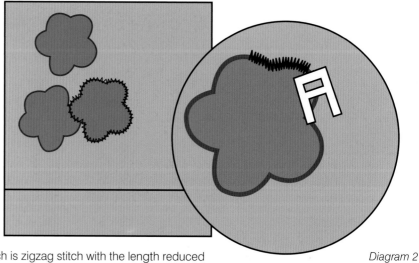

Diagram 2

3 Set your machine for satin stitch, which is zigzag stitch with the length reduced to 0.5mm (60) and the width to 2.5. Stitch around the flower heads using thread to coordinate with the flower fabric. Where the flowers overlap, stitch round the overlapping flower first (see Diagram 2). To curve around the petal shapes smoothly, stop with the needle down to the right (in the towel), pivot the towel a little and continue. At the inner curves, stop with the needle in the flower and pivot.

Diagram 3

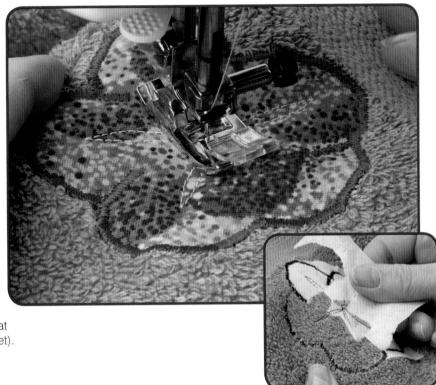

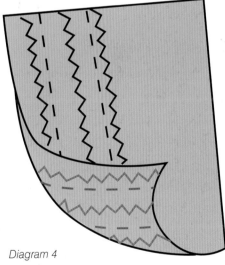

4 Change to the thread that contrasts with the flower fabric and set the machine to straight stitch. Starting at the centre of a flower, stitch a curve out towards the petal edge, pivot with the needle down and stitch a curve back to to the centre. Repeat for all the petals, finishing at the centre again (see Diagram 3). Tear away the stabiliser at the back when you have finished (see inset).

Bobbin work

5 Hand wind a bobbin with the crochet yarn or embroidery thread. Drop the bobbin into the bobbin case but do not pull the thread through the tension. Leave it laying on top of the bobbin. Thread the needle with regular thread.

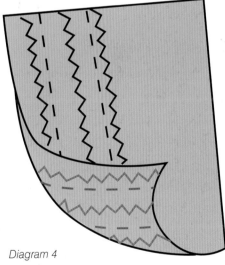

Diagram 4

6 Select zigzag stitch and increase the length to 2.5mm (13) and the width to 3.5 if possible. Place the towel under the presser foot with the right side of the towel facing down towards the throat plate. Working slowly, stitch a row of zigzag stitch. From the top it is stitched with normal thread, but underneath (the right side) you have the wonderful thicker thread. Stitch slowly and check the other side of the work as you go.

7 Do a few more rows, alternating between zigzag and straight stitch, as in Diagram 4 above.

A pair of finished guest towels and a matching face cloth also featuring bobbin work.

ADVANCED
TECHNIQUES

PLEATS

Pleats are simply folds in the fabric which are used to provide shaping or design detail. Because they are created by fabric folds, extra fabric across the width is needed, the amount of which depends on the number and size of the pleats. Tucks are similar to pleats but are generally narrower and are sewn in place close to the folded edge. Pleats tend to be sewn at the top, or part way down only.

There are three main types of pleat, shown below:

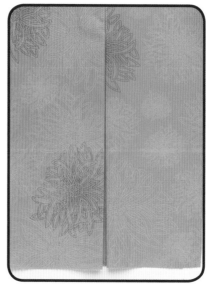

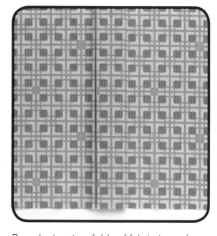

Knife pleats – straight pleats, all facing in the same direction.

Inverted pleats – two straight pleats turned towards each other to form a V opening. Note that if you turn an inverted pleat over you will see that the back is a box pleat.

Box pleats – two folds of fabric turned away from each other to form a flat panel in the centre.

It is always a good idea to finish the hem of a project before adding the pleats if at all possible as it is easier to create a straight hem from a flat piece of fabric.

Making a pleat template

If making a series of pleats that are to be the same size, first make a card template the width of the finished pleat, for instance, 3cm (1¼in) wide. Write along the two long edges, marking one with a placement line and the other with a fold line. Place the template on the fabric to be pleated and transfer the markings to the fabric. It is a good idea to use a different coloured pin or chalk for the fold and placement lines so they are easy to identify. For unpressed pleats, mark down the length of the pleat by 5–10cm (2–4in). For crisp pressed pleats, mark the whole pleat length.

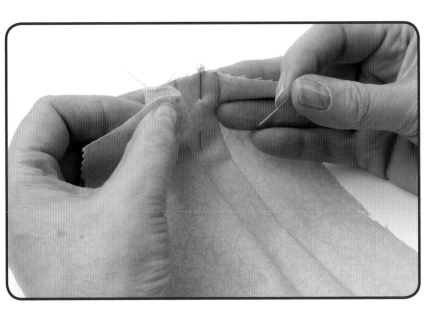

Make a fold at the first fold line and bring the fold to the first placement line – keeping the upper edges of the fabric even. Pin in position along the top edge. Repeat to pin as many pleats as required.

Tips

- Always press with a press cloth to avoid leaving fold imprints on the fabric.

- To keep pleats in place, working from the wrong side, machine stitch close to the inner fold (see right).

- For crisp, even pleats, mark the pleat fold line and placement lines and then fuse iron-on slotted waistbanding to the wrong side with the slotted holes in line with the fold line of the pleat.

TUCKS

Tucks are similar to knife pleats but take less fabric. They are often used for shaping as well as providing a decorative detail. Pin tucks (see page 92) take up very little fabric, but regular tucks can take up a considerable amount across the width, so it is advisable to make the tucks before cutting a piece to the final size.

Tucks are usually marked in line with the straight of the grain, parallel to the selvedges. Vertical tucks are generally pressed away from the centre while horizontal tucks are pressed downwards.

If you are making a series of tucks that are to be evenly spaced, create a little card template as for pleats (see page 109).

Decorative tucks

Use an overcast foot and overcast stitch to stitch the tuck along the folded edge. Place the fold of the fabric butted against the protruding bar on the foot. Most of the overcast stitch is to the left of the bar with regular swings to the right and over the edge of the fabric. Do try out the whole sequence by turning the balance wheel by hand first to ensure the needle doesn't hit the foot at all. A contrast thread will really make them stand out.

Twisted tucks

Stitch a series of tucks vertically. Then press them all in one direction and stitch horizontally across from left to right. Next, starting from the right side, stitch again, about 3–4cm (1¼–1½in) below the first horizontal line of stitching, while pushing the tucks in the opposite direction. Continue doing this from left to right with the tucks pressed flat and from right to left with the tucks pushed in the other direction. The result will be a diamond tucked panel.

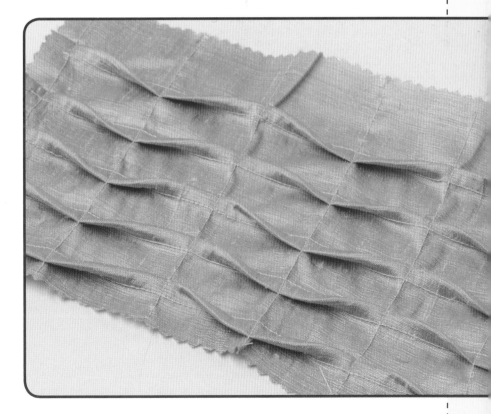

TRIMS

Trims, ribbons and fringing can be added to enhance a project, provide design detail and the 'wow' factor.

Sewing trims in place

If the trim is over 13mm (½in) wide, it is advisable to stitch down both long edges, stitching both in the same direction. Choose a thread that matches the trim and stitch with a straight stitch. If the trim is under 13mm (½in) wide, it can be stitched with a single line of stitching down the centre. Use a zigzag stitch in a matching thread, or in a contrast thread to make the stitching part of the design.

If adding trims to a project, add them before sewing the side seams so that the trim ends can be hidden within the seam. If sewing trims as surface decoration, the ends will need to be neatened by turning them under before attaching the trim.

Mark placement lines in chalk so that you have a line to follow.

Mitring corners

Mitre the trim at the corners for a crisp, neat edge.

1 Stitch the trim in position along both long edges, until you get to the place you want to turn the corner. Fold the trim back on itself and then again along the new stitching line. Press.

2 Unfold the trim so it is just back on itself again and stitch along the diagonal crease. If you are using a bulky trim, cut away the excess under the diagonal stitching.

3 Fold the trim back along the second placement line again and continue stitching along both long edges.

Beaded trims

Beaded trims are often added along hemlines as surface trims or sewn in with the seam so that only the beading is visible from the right side. If stitched within seam, remove any beads in the seam allowance by crushing them. Do not cut the thread holding the beads, as lots more may fall off.

Attaching a beaded trim on top.

A beaded trim in seam.

Lace trims

As well as being attached as a surface trim, lace can be inserted into a fabric panel as a decorative design feature. In this case, it is sewn on the surface of the fabric and then the fabric is cut away from behind.

1 Pin the lace, right side up, on top of the fabric in the position desired.

2 Machine stitch around the edge of the lace. For scalloped edge lace, stitch just inside the curves so the scallop edging remains free.

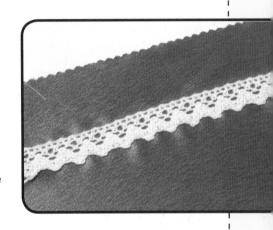

3 Turn the fabric to the wrong side and carefully cut away the fabric between the two rows of stitching, leaving a 6mm (¼in) seam allowance around the edges.

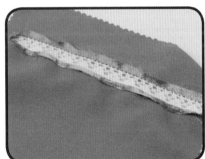

4 Press the seam allowance towards the fabric along the stitching lines.

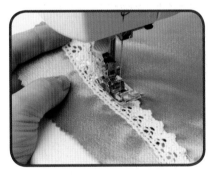

5 Turn the work to the right side again and then edge stitch close to the folded edges of fabric, through all layers (top stitch close to the edge). Stitch in the same direction as before. Finish by trimming back the seam allowance close to this second row of stitching.

COUCHING

Another surface decoration that looks fabulous is couching or gimping. This is when thicker yarns or fine ribbons are laid on the surface and stitched in place. You can get couching feet to feed the yarns evenly spaced under the presser foot and needle or you can guide them by hand. A couching foot will have tunnels or holes in it through which one three, five or seven yarns can be fed.

A couching foot.

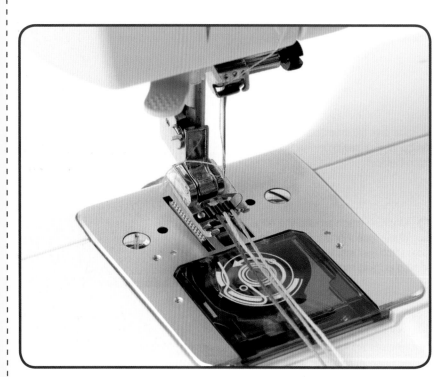

A couching foot with three yarns feeding through it, shown without fabric for clarity.

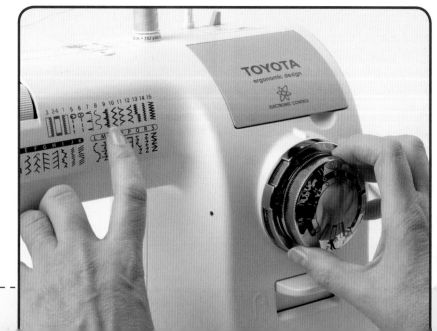

1 Use a triple zigzag stitch to anchor the threads in place. Adjust the width so that it goes either side of the yarn or ribbon.

2 Lay the yarns in the position where you wish to couch them, and hold them at the back with your left hand and at the front with your right. Use the triple zigzag stitch to sew them in position, either using a thread that matches your yarns, or one that contrasts with them for a bold statement.

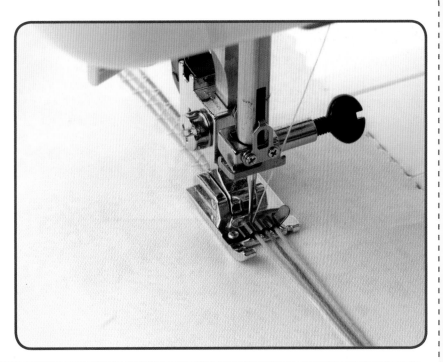

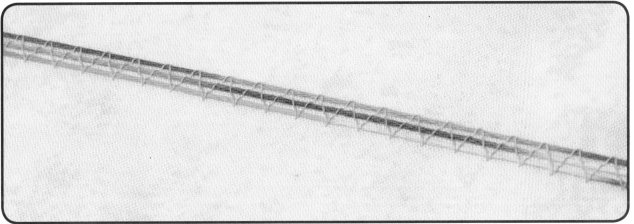

Tip

If you do not have a couching foot, feed the yarns through a straw taped in front of your sewing machine in line with the needle. Alternatively put the thread reels in a pot in front of the machine.

Above: *couching done with a couching foot and below, with a straw. The couching foot separates the yarns so that they are couched down in spaced parallel lines rather than lying together.*

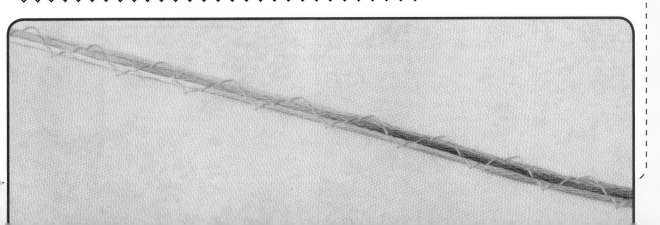

PATCH POCKETS

Patch pockets are attached to the surface of a garment or bag. They don't have to be plain though – they can be shaped, lined and colourful as well as practical. Traditional patch pockets are rectangular or square but they can be virtually any shape. They can be made from the same fabric as the project or a contrast fabric, and they can be lined or unlined. The pocket is created separately and then stitched on to the project.

Self-lined patch pocket

This is an easy pocket to create; you simply cut the pocket twice the length required plus 1.5cm ($^5/_8$in) seam allowances all the way round.

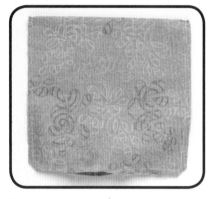

1 With right sides together, fold the pocket in half (the fold will be the top of the pocket). Stitch the side seams and bottom edge, leaving a turning gap in the bottom. Clip the corners at angles, turn through and then press.

2 To create a crisp pocket top, top stitch about 6mm ($^1/_4$in) along the top edge. You can, of course, use a decorative stitch or contrast colour for this. Press the pocket and then place it in position on the project. Edge stitch in place around the sides and bottom 3mm ($^1/_8$in) from the edge. To make sure the top remains securely attached, reverse stitch or create a triangle of stitching at the top edges.

Lined patch pockets

If you are using a main fabric that is heavyweight or bulky (such as fleece or coating) it is better to line the pocket with a lining or cotton fabric. Equally if you wish to make a shaped pocket, it is easier to line it with a separate fabric rather than self-line as above.

To create the pocket, mark out the pocket shape and size on both the main fabric and the lining, adding 1.5cm ($^5/_8$in) seam allowance to the side and bottom edges and 3cm (1¼in) to the top edge.
  Stitch the pocket pieces, right sides together along the top edge only, taking a 6mm (¼in) seam allowance and leaving a turning gap in the middle of the seam. Next mark a fold line 2.5cm (1in) down from the seam and turn the pocket towards the lining along the fold line. Pin and stitch the side seams and bottom edge, including the folded down top, then trim the seam allowances, cutting the corners at an angle close to the stitching. Turn the pocket through the opening left earlier. Slip stitch the opening closed and press the pocket. Top stitch and then edge stitch in place as for self-lined patch pockets.

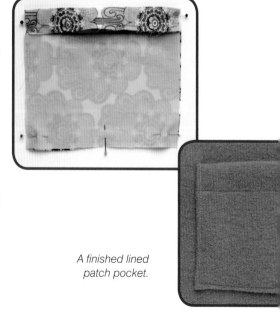

A finished lined patch pocket.

Cargo pocket

Cargo pockets are usually a single layer of fabric (unlined) and have a box pleat in the centre of the pocket which gives it fullness.

1 First determine the length and width of the pocket desired and then add 10cm (4in) to the width in addition to your seam allowances. Find the centre of the width along the top and bottom edges and pin mark. Working with the wrong side uppermost, measure 5cm (2in) either side of the pin mark, fold the fabric at the mark and bring the folds to the centre pin. You have created an inverted pleat. Turn the work over to the right side and you will see a box pleat.

2 Stitch across the pleated fabric to hold it in place and hem the top edge. Neaten all the raw edges of the pocket piece, then turn the edges to the wrong side all the way round the pocket by 1cm (³⁄₈in). Pin and press in place. Position the pocket where desired and edge stitch in place as before.

Shaped pocket

Cut two identical pocket pieces to the shape desired and stitch round the outer edge, leaving a turning gap in one side. Trim the seam allowances, clipping into the seams at curves and close to the V if you are making a heart. Turn through and press with the seams on the edges, tucking the raw edges of the turning gap to the inside. Stitch the pocket to the garment as before, effectively closing the turning gap at the same time as you edge stitch the pocket in position.

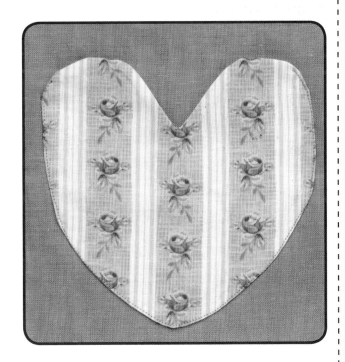

USEFUL INFORMATION

Calculating fabric requirements

Sometimes the fabric width of your chosen fabric is not listed on the pattern envelope so it is difficult to estimate how much fabric you need to purchase. Use this handy conversion guide to take the guesswork out of the decision!

If a pattern calls for 2.30m (2½ yards) of 90cm (36in) wide fabric and your chosen fabric is 115cm (45in) wide, look under the 90cm amount until you find 2.30, then look along that row until you find the amount listed under the 115cm column. The amount of fabric required at the different width is noted here: 1.95m. The imperial amounts are listed in separate columns, which work in the same way.

Tip

Unusual patterns, one-way designs and with nap fabrics may affect the amount needed. Check with your fabric retailer.

90cm wide	36in wide	115cm wide	45in wide	140cm wide	54in wide	150cm wide	60in wide
1.60	1¾	1.30	1⅜	1.05	1⅛	0.95	1
1.85	2	1.50	1⅝	1.30	1⅜	1.15	1¼
2.10	2¼	1.60	1¾	1.50	1½	1.30	1⅜
2.30	2½	1.95	2⅛	1.60	1¾	1.50	1⅝
2.65	2⅞	2.10	2¼	1.75	1⅞	1.60	1¾
2.90	3⅛	2.30	2½	1.85	2	1.75	1⅞
3.10	3⅜	2.55	2¾	2.10	2¼	1.85	2
3.45	3¾	2.65	2⅞	2.20	2⅜	2.10	2¼
3.90	4¼	2.90	3⅛	2.40	2⅝	2.20	2⅜
4.15	4½	3.10	3⅜	2.55	2¾	2.40	2⅝
4.35	4¾	3.35	3⅝	2.65	2⅞	2.55	2¾
4.60	5	3.55	3⅞	2.90	3⅛	2.65	2⅞

TROUBLESHOOTING

Unfortunately, sometimes things do go wrong, but with the handy hints and timely tips on the following pages, there is no reason why you can't be up and sewing again in no time.

Ways to avoid problems

• Clean out the bobbin race regularly – after every sewing session, or more frequently if stitching fabrics that fray and fluff a lot, such as fleece or fur fabrics. Fluff in the works can prevent the bobbin working properly, prevent the needle thread linking up with the bobbin thread and more.

• Change needles regularly. If you are unsure what type of needle is in the machine, replace it.

Tip
Use nail varnish to colour code any needles you can reuse such as embroidery, jeans or twin needles you've only used for a small project. That way you will easily see which type of needle it is.

• Avoid using cheap 'market' threads – they will break easily. Also throw away any old threads that have been saved for years, as they may have weakened over time.

• Make sure the presser foot is raised and the needle is in the highest position when threading the machine as this releases the tension discs and enables the threads to slip through them easily.

• When changing the stitch pattern or the presser foot, make sure the needle is raised as it moves from side to side and may be damaged if it is lowered into the machine. Also try out the stitch by turning the balance wheel by hand to ensure the needle goes through the foot and throat plate without hitting either of them. If it does hit them, check the correct foot is being used and that the needle is not bent.

PROBLEM	SOLUTIONS

Skipped or broken stitches

If the thread isn't feeding smoothly and evenly, it can result in skipped and even broken stitching.

- Rethread the machine, making sure the presser foot is raised first.
- Ensure the thread reel is held in place with a thread retainer. Otherwise the thread reel bounces up and down on the spindle as you stitch, or might get wrapped tightly around the spindle, all of which can cause uneven stitching, skipped stitching or even broken threads.
- Check that the bobbin is inserted the right way up. For drop-in bobbins this is easily seen as there is a printed guide on how the thread should come off the bobbin – usually anticlockwise from the lower left towards the right, then pulled back towards the left through the groove on the casing. Then leave it to be picked up by the needle thread when the balance wheel is turned to take a stitch.
- Defluff the bobbin race. There is a little brush in the machine's tool kit for this purpose.
- Make sure the needle is inserted the right way round (usually with the flat part of the shank facing the back of the machine) and is fully inserted into the holder. Tighten the needle with a screwdriver so it can't work loose.
- Try a new needle. A blunt needle, or one with a tiny burr in the eye (invisible to the naked eye) can shred or break the thread as it travels through at speed.
- Make sure the needle is suited to the fabric. Too large or heavyweight a needle can cause skipped stitches or leave holes in lightweight fabric, while on heavy fabrics or multiple layers, a more robust needle is advisable. Embroidery and jeans needles tend to have larger eyes which can take thicker thread. If sewing with metallic threads, use a metallic needle which has a coated eye to prevent the thread shredding as it passes quickly through the needle eye.
- Stretchy fabric often needs to stretch even once sewn, so stitch with a flexible stitch such as a stretch stitch or small zigzag stitch. This will stretch with the fabric, whereas a straight stitch will break.

Stitching looks wrong

A perfect stitch has the top thread on the right side of the fabric and the bobbin thread on the underside. If the bobbin thread is visible on the right side or the top thread is visible on the underside, try these steps.

- First rethread both bobbin and top thread before making any machine adjustments. Sometimes it is simply a threading problem.
- Having checked threading, check the stitch length/width is suitable for the fabric type. Use small stitches for lightweight fabric and longer stitches for heavier weight fabric.
- If the bobbin thread is visible on the right side, or the top thread on the underside, alter the tension very slightly, a little at a time until the stitches are forming properly. Turn the dial to the right to tighten it (to a higher number) and to the left to loosen it (to a lower number).
- Check the needle type you are using is compatible with the fabric, i.e. a ballpoint needle with stretch fabric, a fine sharps needle with lightweight fabrics, and an embroidery needle for concentrated machine embroidery designs.

PROBLEM

SOLUTIONS

Bent or broken needles

This can have various causes and the solutions for each are shown:

- The needle hitting the side of the presser foot or throat plate. Turn the balance wheel by hand through the stitch pattern to ensure the needle clears the foot and throat plate properly. Remember when changing stitch selection, always make sure the needle is raised first.

- The needle is too fine for the fabric thickness. A fine needle will have trouble penetrating multiple layers or a very dense, heavy fabric. Use a jeans needle or one size 110 (18).

- The needle is blunt. A blunt needle can snag fabric, have trouble penetrating layers or simply catch and break. Change needles every eight hours of sewing or after every project.

- The needle works loose. It will then wobble as it stitches, causing it to bend, or hit the side of the throat plate. Make sure you secure the needle in place by tightening the retaining screw with the screwdriver.

- The thread is getting caught on the spindle and pulling tight. If not noticed in time, this can lead to the needle being bent or broken. Make sure you use a thread retainer to prevent the reel bouncing up and down on the spindle.

The tension looks wrong

- Check that it is set on the 'regular' tension. This is usually marked in some way by darker or different coloured numbers, or lines linking the average tension.

- Use the same thread in the top and bobbin or adjust the tension to compensate for a thicker/thinner thread top or bottom.

- Clean out the bobbin race.

- If none of the above works and you have changed the needle and rethreaded completely, take the machine to a service engineer for a service or timing adjustment.

Seams are puckering

- Check that the tension is on the regular setting. Rethread the machine with the same thread in the top and bobbin.

- Use the right stitch length to suit the fabric: 2.2–2.5mm (13) for lightweight fabrics and 2.5–3.0mm (9) for heavyweight fabrics or multiple layers.

- Check that you have the right needle for the fabric being stitched: fine sharps needles for lightweight fabric; robust jeans needles for heavyweight fabrics.

PROBLEM	SOLUTIONS
Threads loop or bunch on the underside of the fabric at the start of a seam	• Hold the thread ends in your left hand towards the back for the first few stitches. • If the above doesn't solve the problem, rethread the machine, making sure the presser foot is raised. Check the tension is on the 'regular' setting.
Fabric not feeding through or getting caught in the feed dogs	• Make sure the feed dogs are raised and working (turn the balance wheel by hand to see them raise and lower as the needle goes up and down. If they do not, check that the machine has not been left set up for free-motion stitching with the feed dogs lowered. Check the manual to see how to raise or lower the feed dogs. • When working with delicate fabrics, place a scrap of soluble stabiliser under the seam at the start to prevent the fabric being pulled into the feed dogs. Start the seam 2cm (¾in) from the end, reverse stitch and then go forwards again. • If available, use a straight stitch throat plate which has a smaller hole for the feed dogs and needle, thus preventing fine fabrics being pulled into the feed dogs.
Threads keep breaking	• Rethread the machine, making sure the presser foot is raised. Check that the thread is coming off the reel smoothly and not getting caught on the spindle. • Use good quality thread, since cheap threads will split and break easily. Avoid using very old threads that might have weakened over the years. • If the bobbin thread keeps breaking, check that the bobbin race is clear of fluff and lint.
Thread pulls out of the needle at the start of a seam	• Make sure you have a long enough thread tail at the start of a seam to prevent it pulling back up and out of the needle as you start to sew.

PROBLEM	SOLUTIONS
Fabric jammed under the presser foot This may be caused by a build-up of fluff in the bobbin race, fabric being pulled into the throat plate or a bobbin that is nearly out of thread and what is left getting wrapped around the race.	• Raise and if possible remove the presser foot, remove the needle and pull away. Gently ease out the fabric and snip the threads below. • Clean out the bobbin race and rethread. • Check the bobbin is wound properly.
Needle threader not working Caused by the needle eye not being in line with threader hook or the hook being damaged or broken.	• Raise the needle to the highest position and check it is in the centre position. • Replace the needle. • Go to a service engineer to replace the needle threader hook or straighten the hook.
Odd noise and machine jamming Can be caused by thread, lint or fluff caught in the race hook or a pin caught in the machine.	• Carefully remove all threads and fluff from the bobbin race and clean the feed dogs and race hook. • If a pin is lodged in the mechanism, consult a service engineer.
Machine not working	• Check that it is turned on. • Check there is no thread tangled in the race area. • Make sure the bobbin winder is not in the winding position or that the section of the balance wheel is back in the sewing position.
One-step buttonhole not working	• Make sure the buttonhole lever (left back of machine) is lowered.

Tip
It is rarely necessary to alter tensions on modern machines and a small alteration to tighten or loosen the tension goes a long way, so adjust very slowly, a little at a time.

Tip
Keep your sewing machine box and inner packaging for transporting the machine to the service engineer.

GLOSSARY

Appliqué A fabric shape or motif that is attached to the surface of a base fabric. Reverse appliqué is when the extra shape is attached to the back of the main fabric, which is then cut away to reveal the appliqué fabric.

Basting (tacking) Temporary stitching to hold layers together before seaming. Basting can be done by hand or machine (using the longest stitch length available). Use a contrast colour thread, so it can be removed easily later.

Bias The bias or bias cut is the most stretchy part of the fabric; garments cut on the bias drape beautifully. Bias binding will curve round corners easily. The true bias is 45 degrees to the straight of the grain.

Bias binding A fabric strip that is cut on the bias and folded so that it can be wrapped round raw edges to encase and neaten them.

Bobbin fill A very fine thread used in the bobbin when sewing machine-embroidered designs with concentrated stitching. Generally available in black or white.

Clipping and notching This is a method to help seams lay flat when turned through to the right side. Seam allowances are clipped or notched at curved areas. Clip inner curves by snipping close to the stitching with diagonal snips. Notch outer curves by cutting little wedges from the seam allowance.

Couching (gimping) This is a technique to attach threads or cords to the surface of a fabric. The threads are laid on the surface and couched down with a stitch such as triple zigzag stitch.

Cutting line Commercial patterns have a bold outer line which is the line to follow when cutting out. The seam or stitching lining is then 6–15mm (¼–⅝in) away.

Darts These are used to add shape to garments or to take out fullness. Single darts are folds of fabric that taper from the fold at the fabric edge to narrow points. Double darts have a wide centre, narrowing to points at either end (these are used for waist darts). Sew from the widest edge to the point and fix the stitches on the spot or tie off the threads (do not reverse stitch).

Ease Every garment needs some ease in it for movement when wearing. This added ease is included in pattern pieces. Designers may also add design ease to create a loose style of garment. To check how much ease is included, refer to the finished garment measurements on the pattern and compare these with body measurements.

Ease stitch This is used to fit a slightly longer piece of fabric to a shorter one to create shape in a garment (for instance, for princess seams or to insert set-in sleeves into an armhole). Ease stitch is sewn just within the seam allowance with a slightly longer stitch length.

Edge stitching This is top stitching, visible on the outside of a project, that is stitched a scant 2–3mm (⅛in) from the edge. It is particularly useful when attaching patch pockets or surface trims.

Feed dogs These are the jagged teeth that protrude through the throat plate under the needle. They move up and down in time with the needle to help feed the fabric through as it is stitched.

Free-motion stitching When the feed dogs are lowered out of the way, you can move the fabric in any direction you like as you stitch – this is known as free motion or free-hand machine stitching.

Grain/grain line Woven fabrics have a grain: the vertical warp threads are the straight grain, and the horizontal weft threads are the crosswise grain. Commercial patterns often have a grain line printed on them – this has to be parallel to the selvedge of the fabric so that the piece is cut on the 'straight of grain' which in turn ensures it hangs properly.

Ham A stuffed, ham-shaped pressing aid that is use to press areas that need to remain curved such as the tops of sleeves or darts.

Interfacing An additional layer of fabric or specialist material that is attached to the reverse of the fabric to provide support and strength. Special interfacing fabrics can be sew-in or iron-on with a fusible backing. Interfacing is used on areas such as waistbands, collars, cuffs and facings.

Nap The surface texture on a fabric which makes it look different from different angles. Pattern pieces must be cut in the same direction on a napped fabric.

Notions The items required to complete a garment or project including interfacing, zips, buttons and elastic.

Overcast/overedge stitch A special stitch created on the edge of the fabric to neaten the raw edge and prevent fraying. A regular zigzag stitch can also be used to overcast the seam allowance.

Pattern match This term is used most often in curtain making. It describes the technique of matching fabric designs on pieces that are to be joined. You may also want to pattern match checks or stripes on garments. To do so, cut one piece on a single layer of fabric, then place this cut piece next to the remaining fabric so the next section can be placed to match the pattern at key points (on garments this may be the bust or hips). When cutting two of the same pattern piece, the second one should be placed face down on the fabric to ensure a left and right.

Pattern notches Commercial patterns have triangular wedge-shaped notches marked on the cutting line. These are used to match up corresponding pieces for front to back, collars to neck edge etc. Cut out around notches rather than into the seam allowance to prevent unnecessary fraying.

Pilling Also known as bobbling, this term describes the tiny fabric balls that build up after repeated wash and wear. Remove them with a fabric shaver.

Press cloth A cloth used to protect the main project fabric when pressing. Cotton organza makes a very good press cloth as it can withstand high temperatures and is transparent so you can see where you are pressing. Press every seam before sewing over it again to embed the stitching and produce a flat seam.

Pressing The method of ironing used in sewing terms. Pressing differs from regular ironing as you don't simply glide the iron back and forth, rather you lower it to the fabric, hold, lift and lower again. Press seams from the reverse side or use a press cloth when pressing from the right side.

Quilting Stitching that is used to hold fabric layers together.

Satin stitch A very close zigzag stitch used to cover raw edges of appliqués or create letters. A regular zigzag stitch can be altered by decreasing the stitch length to bring the stitches close together. A length of 0.3–0.5mm (60) will create a lovely close stitch, covering the fabric edges completely.

Seam allowance This is the amount of fabric between the stitching line and the cut edge. A seam allowance is needed to prevent the seams pulling apart during wear. It must be neatened to prevent fraying, using an overcast stitch, zigzag stitch or pinking shears.

Selvedge (selvage) The finished side edges of fabric. They are often more tightly woven so should be cut off when cutting out pattern pieces.

Sew-through button A button with two or four holes through which you sew to attach the button to a garment.

Shank button A button with a loop on the underside through which you sew to attach it to the main fabric. The raised loop ensures there is space between button and fabric so that when bulky fabric is buttoned, it will lay flat.

Stabiliser A bonded material which is used to back a fabric while it is being sewn with decorative stitching or embroidery, in order to provide support and prevent puckering or unwanted stretching. Stabilisers may be tear-away, soluble (wash-away) or heat-away. Once stitching is complete, they are removed.

Stay stitching Use a regular stitch length and stitch just within the seam allowance on all curved areas such as necklines, to prevent the fabrics stretching during handling and seaming.

Stitch in the ditch This technique is worked from the right side of a project. It is a row of stitching that is formed along the previous seam so that it is virtually invisible. It is used to secure facings, casings and hem edges. Use a slightly longer than normal stitch length (3– 3.5mm/9) and with right side up, insert the needle in the ditch created by the previous seam.With your hands either side of the needle, gently pull the fabric apart to open up the ditch slightly and continue stitching, removing pins as you go and catching the facing in place on the wrong side.

Toile (muslin) A test garment made in a cheap cloth such as calico or cotton to check for fit before making up a garment in expensive fabric.

Top stitching Stitching that is visible on the right side of a project. It can be regular stitch length, in a thread colour to match the fabric, or in a bolder thread and a contrast colour. It is often used to hold facings in place, or finish a hem.

Warp These are the threads put on the loom first before a fabric is woven. The weft threads are then woven between them from side to side.

Weft The threads making up the filling yarns of a woven fabric.

Welt The visible part of the binding on a buttonhole or pocket opening.

INDEX